TEACHING YOURSELF TO TEACH

A COMPREHENSIVE GUIDE TO THE FUNDAMENTAL
AND PRACTICAL INFORMATION YOU NEED TO
SUCCEED AS A TEACHER TODAY

SELENA WATTS

CONTENTS

This lesson plan checklist includes:

- The 10 essential elements of a lesson plan that will help you teach with complete confidence.
- High-quality items that you can use to help you get the most from your students.
- Where you can buy these items for the lowest price.

The last thing we want is for your lessons to be less than perfect because you weren't prepared.

To receive your essential 10-point lesson planning checklist, simply scan the QR code below:

INTRODUCTION: LEARNING HOW TO TEACH

"I never teach my pupils; I only attempt to provide the conditions in which they can learn."

— EINSTEIN

Do you know what it means to be a truly great teacher?

Some people believe that teaching is merely an occupation while others think that it's one of the easiest things a person can do with their life. But the truth is, teaching requires passion, commitment, and an unending journey of learning. To become a truly enlightened and inspiring teacher, there is a lot you must learn.

Whether you are already a teacher by profession or you are thinking about becoming a teacher in the future, this book will be extremely valuable to you. As a teacher myself, I am still in the process of learning and with each lesson I learn, I realize how noble being a teacher is. When I was young, I didn't want to become a teacher. Although my teachers knew exactly how to inspire me while I was still in school, I never thought that my future involved educating others.

And yet, here I am.

I have been teaching for years now and I still see it as one of life's greatest adventures. The best part about being a teacher is that you can actually learn how to become better at it. As long as you have an open mind about learning, you can keep improving yourself as time goes by. Of course, since you are a teacher, learning should be the easiest thing for you!

In this book, you will learn everything you need to become a better teacher. From learning all about your students to discovering the most effective teaching strategies, there is so much knowledge to unlock and this book is your key. Since I am also a teacher like you, I understand exactly what kind of challenges you are going through. I have firsthand experience with the most challenging types of students in class.

Through research and a lot of trial-and-error, I learned how to deal with them in the most effective ways possible. I have tried being the new teacher in a school where it seemed like all of my colleagues were so much better than me. So, I encouraged myself to grow and improve until I could become just like them. Some of them said that I became even better and this made my heart swell with joy.

My journey towards becoming the best teacher I can be is still ongoing. But I have learned enough to share with people like you who want to become better too. In this book, you will learn all about learning styles—one of the most important things you need to know if you want to meet the needs of your students. You will also learn all about blended learning, how to deal with classroom disruptions, the effectiveness of classroom management, the most realistic ways to motivate your students, and so much more. By the end of this book, you will have more confidence in your teaching abilities, as well as, your capacity to meet the expectations of your students.

With all of these benefits, you might be wondering who I am and why you should continue reading. If I were in your place, I would be wondering the same thing so before we continue with your journey of teaching yourself to teach, let me share my story with you first.

As I have already mentioned, I am a teacher just like you. The confidence and passion I have to write this book come from the many years of teaching I've had. Although I was perfectly comfortable with the traditional teaching methods, I had to keep up with the times. I admit that in the beginning, I struggled with virtual learning. But since these were the new methods that caught the attention of students, I strove to make them part of my own teaching procedures too.

Before writing this book, I had gained experience in both real-life and virtual teaching environments. Through the years, I have also spent a lot of time testing and exploring different teaching strategies to find what works and what doesn't. Now, I am passionate about sharing my knowledge with you and with all other teachers who want to become the best versions of themselves as they practice their craft.

While I embarked on a journey of discovery, I developed a profound sense of care for my students. I care deeply about making sure that students get all the benefits they need in school. Also, I strongly believe that all teachers should try everything they can to provide their students with the best learning experience. Just like you—and probably all other teachers in the world—I met the same challenges. I didn't understand the terminology used by teachers (and students) and I struggled greatly with creating courses to keep my students engaged and motivated. As I overcame these challenges, I realized that teachers must possess a number of essential skills and qualities to become the best. And you can develop these through learning, practice, and even through failure.

You read that right—failure. Even if you feel like a failure right now or at any point in your career as a teacher, you should see these experiences as learning opportunities. Through failure, you learn how to become better and with the right learning tools (such as this book), you can inspire yourself to keep moving forward. To put things simply, I am a teacher with a passion to help you resolve the pain or frustration you are experiencing. Instead of giving up or giving in to the negative experiences you have, I want to help you discover the strength you have within until you achieve the teaching goals you have set for yourself.

This isn't just a book about teaching. It is a valuable resource that you will use to become an amazing, inspiring, and genuine teacher. Whether you are teaching young children, college students or those in between, you can apply everything you will learn here. Similarly, whether you are using traditional teaching methods, you're a teacher of a virtual class or you need both, this book will help you learn everything you need to shine.

If you're ready to start improving yourself, keep reading so that we can begin!

1

GETTING TO KNOW YOUR STUDENTS

D id you know that there are different types of learners?

As a teacher, you may have already heard about learning styles and the different types of learners. But to become the best teacher you can be, you should be aware of the types of learners you have in your class. This awareness helps you come up with the best approach to teaching them and giving them the most effective learning experiences ever.

If you accept that all students are different, you should also learn to accept that students process information differently too. You might have students who listen well but aren't able to catch obvious details when given visual exercises. You might have students who shine when working with others and those who prefer to work on their own. And here's the challenge—in a single class, you might have students who are vastly different in terms of their learning styles. But if you can find ways to cater to the needs of these different students, then you will find success in your teaching goals.

All students have a dominant learning style. These learning styles will help you determine the best ways in which your students can learn. The different learning styles are:

- Auditory Learners
- Kinesthetic Learners
- Logical Learners
- Naturalistic Learners
- Read + Write Learners
- Social Learners
- Solitary Learners
- Verbal Learners
- Visual Learners

As a teacher, it is your job to discover your students' individual learning styles. You can do this through observation, interaction, and having adequate knowledge about the different learning styles. If you aren't familiar with these learning styles, you won't be able to determine what kind of learners your students are. Even if you are extremely observant or you have built a strong connection with your students, knowing all about the different learning styles is key.

In this first chapter, you will discover the different learning styles, the characteristics of learners, and practical tips to help you cater to the needs of these learners. Here, you will gain a better understanding of what learning styles truly mean and how you can give your students what they need even if you have a class that consists of different learners. Coming up with activities and lesson plans will become much easier when you know the types of learners you need to teach. The best part is, even after familiarizing yourself with these learning styles, you can keep coming back to this book and use it as a reference while creating your lesson plans!

DIFFERENT STROKES FOR DIFFERENT FOLKS

Understanding what learning styles are will help you no matter what age your students are in. You can even use your knowledge of learning styles to help you improve as a teacher. For instance, if you discover that you are a visual learner, then you can use visual tools to help you learn new concepts and skills. But if you think that you are more of an auditory learner, then you may want to play audiobooks and similar resources while you are doing other activities. By practicing the application of learning style strategies on yourself, you will find it easier to apply these strategies to your students too.

When you truly understand the concept of learning styles, you will be able to plan your classes more effectively too. For instance, if you have several social learners in your class, then you can have a lot of group activities. If your class consists mostly of kinesthetic learners, having physical activities would make your lessons livelier and more effective. These are just some examples of how you can use your knowledge of learning styles to improve your teaching.

If you have been reading about learning styles in the past, you might have noticed that most psychological and teaching handbooks claim that there are four types of learners. These claims have stemmed from the VARK model by Neil Fleming. According to this model, the learning styles of students vary and these depend on a number of cognitive, emotional, and environmental factors. Since each student is unique, discovering the learning styles of your students will enable you to develop strategies, lessons, and activities that incorporate the various learning styles for the different learners in your class. Understanding the VARK model will help you do this.

The term VARK stands for visual, auditory, reading + writing, and kinesthetic. These are the basic learning styles but these days, there are many more. The VARK model focuses on the concept of students processing and retaining information in different ways. Also, this model focuses on the idea that students have their own "preferred learning modes" that enable them to learn things in the most effective ways possible. When it comes to the VARK model, there are two key things to remember:

1. The learning styles of students have a significant impact on how they learn and how they behave.
2. When students can access or learn information through their preferred learning modes, they are more motivated, and they understand concepts more.

Therefore, as a teacher, you should try to match your teaching strategies with the learning styles of your students to make them feel more comfortable and confident in your class. When you understand the types of learners you have in your class, you can gain a clearer perspective of the kind of study techniques and learning activities to include in your lesson plans.

Right now, take a moment to think about the students in your class. As a teacher, you may confidently say that you already "know your students." You know their names, you're familiar with their interests, you know how they behave in class, and you might even know how most of them learn. While all of this information is valuable, it is quite basic. If you want to maximize the learning in your class, you need to keep learning about your students until you discover exactly how they learn.

Trying to imagine how you can teach a class of different types of learners can seem overwhelming—although it doesn't have to be. The great thing about teaching is that it's extremely flexible and versatile. Before moving on to the different learning styles, let me share some of the basic teaching approaches that you can use no matter what types of learners you have:

1. Student-Based

When you use this approach, you will make your students the main focus of your teaching. Instead of always being the teacher of the class, you will give your students a chance to express themselves through activities like reporting and sharing, for example. Also, you might regularly ask your students to provide input to help you with your teaching strategies. In other words, you will only serve as their guide or facilitator in the classroom. This is a very effective approach for different types of learners.

2. Cooperative

This is a variation of the first approach wherein you would focus on your students' social growth apart from their academics. The cooperative approach involves a lot of group work, collaboration, and even peer evaluation. This is an excellent approach if you have a class of students who are familiar with one another. Even if you have different learners in the class, they can help each other cope as you give them activities that encourage interaction.

3. Teacher-Based

This is the most "traditional" approach to teaching and it still works today. Again, this approach is effective even if you have different learners in your class. However, if you want to be the main focus in your class each day, you must deliver. Plan your lessons well and make sure that everything you say, show, and express in class will catch the attention of your students. Also, find ways to motivate your students so that they will always be willing to listen to you.

4. Inquiry-Based

This teaching style is all about encouraging your students to ask a lot of questions. It's meant to inspire independence and profound learning through hands-on activities. Just like the student-based approach, you will serve as a guide and a facilitator in the class instead of a teacher.

5. Mixed Approach

By far, this is the most innovative teaching style that you can use. Essentially, you would use different styles to teach your students. If you have a group of different learners, this is probably the best style to use. Take the best parts of the other teaching styles and merge them to create an approach that is uniquely you; one that allows you to give your students the best learning experience by giving them varied activities that cater to different learning styles.

Hopefully, these teaching styles will help put your mind at ease when it comes to learning styles. The bottom line is that you don't have to feel stressed just because you found out that you have a class with five or six types of learners. Moreover, most learners have more than one learning style although one of those learning styles is the dominant one. If you can find out all the learning styles of your students, not just the dominant ones, this will be even more helpful to you.

While the VARK model focuses on four basic learning styles, some expert psychologists and educators have expanded the model. Now, they claim that there are more types of learners to be aware of. Now, let's take a look at these different types of learners, their characteristics, and how you can teach such learners.

AUDITORY LEARNERS

Auditory or "aural" learners are the ones who respond well to rhythms, rhymes, music, and sounds. You know that a student is an auditory learner if they remember things that they hear—like conversations or explanations—and they feel an emotional response whenever they hear music. Basically, music and sounds are your best bet when you have learners of this type in your classroom.

Since most auditory learners have a great sense of rhythm, a lot of them turn out to be musicians or singers. When they hear the different sounds of musical instruments, they learn these sounds right away. Since auditory learners are good listeners, they are also the best types of students to attend verbal presentations like speeches or lectures. Here are some other characteristics of auditory learners to look out for so that you can identify them in your class:

- When auditory learners speak with others, you may

hear them use phrases like, "let's talk about me,"
"please tell me" or "explain this to me," for example.

- Auditory learners prefer to learn information through noises, sounds, and spoken words. They learn either by listening or by explaining what they had learned using their own words.
- It's easy for auditory learners to remember instructions that they hear.
- Auditory learners can also remember the lyrics of songs only after listening to the songs a couple of times.
- It's easy for auditory learners to retain information when music is playing in the background. In the same way, they can also remember information better when presented in a rhythmic way.

Simply put, auditory learners are all about learning through listening. Auditory learners are the best types of students for music teachers. Of course, you don't have to be a music teacher to engage your auditory learners in class. No matter what type of learners your students are, you can find ways to teach them effectively. For auditory learners, here are some strategies for you:

- Remember the importance of oral communication. Speak up in class but also give your students a chance to speak. This verbal communication will help them learn more effectively.

- Practice your oral delivery so that you can learn how to speak in lively and engaging ways. This is one tip that can help you teach different types of learners better.

- When telling stories in class, prepare relevant sound effects, and play them while telling your story. Also, use different voices when saying the lines of the different characters.

- Have a lot of activities wherein students have group or class discussions. You can also pair up your students to give them a chance to discuss lessons. In such a case, you can pair auditory learners together. As for the other types of learners, try to pair the ones who complement each other's learning styles.

- When you write information on black or whiteboards, read the information out loud. Or you can also call the auditory learners in your class to read the information aloud.

- Allow your students to record your lessons so that they can listen to the recording after your class. If your students take down notes during your class, encourage them to read their notes out loud when reviewing.

- Assign your auditory learners to seats where they won't be distracted by noises or other students who tend to chat with each other during class.

- Use a lot of rhymes and mnemonic devices to help your students retain information.
- Ask a lot of questions throughout your lesson. At the end of your lesson, ask your students to give an oral summary of what they have learned.
- If you're planning to give your students reading assignments, try to look for books that have audiobook versions.
- Remember that auditory learners enjoy songs, music, following oral instructions, listening to audiotapes, lectures, debates, speeches, stories, auditory repetition, and playing word games.

Aside from using these strategies, you should also know the areas or methods that auditory learners might find challenging. These include:

- Writing activities, especially for younger children who are learning how to form letters.
- Activities that require complete silence for extended periods of time.
- Trying to concentrate when there are distracting background noises.
- Having to follow instructions that you have written on the board.
- Taking written tests that are timed.
- Having to remember faces, details or objects visually.

KINESTHETIC LEARNERS

Kinesthetic or "practical" learners are the ones who respond well when they can use movements in learning. This type of learner is very hands-on, and they love practicing what they learn. Kinesthetic learners use their hands, legs, and other body parts to express themselves which is why physical activities and sports are the best types of activities for them. They love to tinker with things, they usually have superior fine-motor skills, and they learn best when you give them a chance to move or to do other things instead of just listening to you throughout the day.

By nature, kinesthetic learners prefer physical experiences. This means that they learn a lot when holding, touching, doing, feeling, and having hands-on activities. If you frequently hear a student say things like, "how does that feel?" or "can I give it a try?" they're probably a kinesthetic learner. This discovery gives you an opportunity to think of activities that they will appreciate as a kinesthetic learner. Here are some other characteristics of kinesthetic learners to look out for so that you can identify them in your class:

- They prefer to move while they are learning. For younger kids, you might notice them moving around the classroom but when you ask them a question, they can answer you correctly.
- Some kinesthetic learners remember concepts better

when they are walking or pacing around while reciting or reading information.

- Kinesthetic learners are more inclined towards athletic, creative or artsy activities where they can feel involved in the learning process.
- Also, kinesthetic learners typically have a lot of energy which they need to channel towards different things so that they don't end up causing disruptions in class.

Simply put, kinesthetic learners are all about moving and doing. Kinesthetic learners are the best types of students for art or physical education teachers. Of course, you don't have to be these types of teachers to engage your kinesthetic learners in class. For kinesthetic learners, here are some strategies for you:

- Have activities that encourage movement within your lessons.
- Plan activities that include problem-solving or mapping out their thoughts. Such activities might not involve a lot of movement, but they are very hands-on.
- Speaking of hands-on activities, have a lot of these too. Experiments are the best example of hands-on activities. When your kinesthetic learners are involved in the learning process, they learn more effectively.
- Role-play activities are an excellent way to get everyone in your class involved while giving your

kinesthetic learners a chance to get up and move.
Charades is a fun and effective game too.

- Plan activities that involve interacting with
manipulatives or physical objects, solving puzzles, and
drawing maps, diagrams or graphs.
- Allow your students to use different writing materials
when they need to take down notes. This makes the
activity more appealing to them.
- Take breaks once in a while, especially if you planned a
lesson that mainly involves discussions. You can ask
your students to stand and walk around the class or
have simple stretching exercises every twenty minutes
or so. Make sure to incorporate these short breaks into
your lesson plan.
- Once in a while, find a place with a large space to have
your class. Here, do a lot of movement, drawing, and
problem-solving exercises. This is one strategy that all
types of learners will enjoy.
- Encourage your kinesthetic learners (and everyone else
in the class) to declutter their workspaces to avoid
distractions. Otherwise, they might just fiddle with the
objects on their desks instead of listening to you.
- Never punish your students if they keep moving or
fidgeting. This will make them feel restricted or it
might make them feel like you are forcing them to sit
through your class.
- If you are discussing something in class, try to explain

things in terms of feelings or sensations. This will help
your students visualize and understand your
explanations better.

- When it's time for your kinesthetic learners to review
  what they have learned, encourage them to exercise or
  engage in other physical activities while doing so.

Aside from using these strategies, you should also know the
areas or methods that kinesthetic learners might find challenging. These include:

- Interpreting non-verbal cues or communications.
- Expressing themselves verbally without using gestures
  or movements.
- Doing tasks on their own, especially if these tasks don't
  involve any movement.
- Having to write with good spacing and legible
  handwriting, especially in cursive.
- Having to sit still and listen for long periods of time.
- Controlling their natural impulse to move.
- Recalling things that they have heard or seen.

LOGICAL LEARNERS

Logical or "mathematical" learners are the ones who respond
well to reasoning and logic. They are very good at categorizing,
organizing, and classifying information. They are amazing

problem solvers, especially when dealing with mathematical problems. Logical learners are also extremely efficient at analyzing cause-and-effect relationships. If your lessons involve numbers, logic, and reasoning, you will surely see your logical learners shine.

They tend to think scientifically and use their mind to solve complex strategies. When you ask these learners what their favorite subjects are, they will say science, math, and subjects that involve computers. Here are some other characteristics of logical learners to look out for so that you can identify them in your class:

- While learning, logical learners tend to sort, categorize, and classify information to help them understand things better.
- Also, logical learners don't have trouble understanding the relationships between numbers, and recognizing patterns comes easily to them.
- Logical learners love playing games that involve strategic thinking such as backgammon, chess, and other board games.
- Because of how their minds work, logical learners typically grow up to be scientists, engineers, mathematicians, and computer programmers.

Simply put, logical learners are all about learning through logic and reasoning. Logical learners are the best types of students for science and math teachers. Of course, you don't have to be a science or math teacher to engage your logical learners in class. For logical learners, here are some strategies for you:

- While teaching math or science subjects to logical learners is a breeze, they might not be too keen on learning other subjects. But you don't have to get intimidated! There will always be ways for you to engage your learners no matter how disinterested they might seem.
- If you want your logical learners to do art, then you can introduce this subject through a color wheel. You can also introduce art by teaching them the concept of mixing colors.
- If you want your logical learners to learn geography or history, make them feel more interested by including classification taxonomy, statistics, and similar lessons.
- If you want your logical learners to learn literature, ask your students to categorize books by genre.
- If you want your logical learners to learn music, introduce the mathematical relationship that exists between notes. As with literature, you can also ask these learners to classify different musical instruments.
- No matter what subject you want to introduce, try to find ways to make things more systematic and logical. You can even ask your logical learners to help you come up with activities to share with the class.

- Give your logical learners opportunities to interpret information that is both abstract and visual.

- Include a lot of problem-solving activities in your lesson plans and when it's time to work, challenge your logical learners to solve those problems on their own. Exercises that involve critical thinking would be very interesting for them too.

- Allow your students to come up with their own outlines, frameworks, and patterns for the lessons you introduce. This gives them an opportunity to learn at their own pace and use their preferred method.

- If you have to discuss unrelated information, try to find ways to incorporate facts and statistics in the lessons. Then when you're done, ask your students to think of a concluding statement for your lessons.

- If you can't find ways to incorporate fun facts and statistics, focus on the key concepts behind the lessons you're introducing instead.

Aside from using these strategies, you should also know the areas or methods that logical listeners might find challenging. These include:

- Having to participate in an activity that doesn't have any clear structure, guidelines or rules.

- Sitting through lessons that only involve listening to explanations.

- Being forced to deal with illogical or irrational situations in the class. For instance, asking your student to give an extemporaneous speech on a topic that they have no interest in.

NATURALISTIC LEARNERS

Naturalist learners are the ones who respond well when they can experience or work in nature. To understand things, they use scientific knowledge, and to learn, they try to find patterns in nature. This learning style is one of the most recent additions and yet, naturalistic learners have been in existence even before they were labeled as such.

If you have naturalistic learners in your class, you may notice that they are very interested and participative whenever they are outdoors. This is because they use nature to help guide their process of learning. Here are some other characteristics of naturalistic learners to look out for so that you can identify them in your class:

- Whenever naturalistic learners are outside, you can find them observing the different processes in nature.
- If you try sitting with a naturalistic learner while they are observing the outside world, you may get a lot of profound insights.
- Naturalistic learners are completely in tune with nature. This is where they feel comfortable and

this is where they are most willing to learn new things.

- Naturalistic learners use patterns and elements in nature to find solutions to problems and create new things.
- These learners can spot even the smallest changes that happen in their environments, especially if you frequently spend time outdoors.
- They can catalog and categorize information with ease. This makes it easier for them to understand new concepts.
- Their interest is awakened when studying zoology, biology, botany, and other subjects that focus on nature.
- Because of the nature of their preferred learning styles, a lot of naturalistic learners grow up to be horticulturists, scientists, and other occupations that involve things in the natural world.

Simply put, naturalistic learners are all about learning through nature. Naturalistic learners are the best types of students for science teachers. Of course, you don't have to be a science teacher to engage your naturalistic learners in class. For naturalistic learners, here are some strategies for you:

- When planning your lessons, include or schedule some activities that you would have outdoors. All types of learners would appreciate this. Plus, getting some fresh air will do wonders for everyone's health.

- Create a connection with your naturalistic learners by approaching them and starting a conversation while you are outdoors.

- Make it easier for them to learn concepts by connecting the concepts to the natural world. This might be a challenge but with a little creativity, you will help your students learn more effectively. For instance, if you are studying ordinal numbers or sequencing in math, connect this to life cycles where your students would have to arrange the life cycles in the right order.

- You can also use real-life examples that are connected to nature, people or daily life when you're explaining new concepts. For instance, if you're teaching physical education, play some music, and ask your students to join you in imitating the movements of animals.

- Have plenty of experiments in class. Along with this, share some case studies and observational data to make your experiments more interesting.

Aside from using these strategies, you should also know the areas or methods that naturalistic listeners might find challenging. These include:

- Learning new things that have no connection with the real world, with nature or daily life.
- Spending too much time indoors or never having any opportunities to play, explore, observe or learn in nature.
- Writing about topics that they have absolutely no interest in.
- Being spoon-fed when it comes to learning. This means that you just provide all of the information without giving them a chance to discover patterns on their own, for example.

READ + WRITE LEARNERS

Read + write learners are the ones who respond well through reading and writing. For them, written words are the best way to learn new information. For these learners to gain knowledge, they go through different text and study materials. Read + write learners are the best type of learners of the traditional way of teaching. In the past, teachers used to rely heavily on books wherein students would have to keep reviewing the information written in those books until they achieve mastery. Although such a method is still being used, only dominant read + write learners truly benefit from it.

By nature, read + write learners learn most effectively when information is presented to them in the form of words. If you have such learners in your class, you will notice them easily as they excel in written assignments like tests, book reports, and essays, for example. Here are some other characteristics of read + write learners to look out for, so that you can identify them in your class:

- Read + write learners focus on text-based output and input—which means all forms of writing and reading.
- Studying written notes allows these learners to retain information effectively.
- They enjoy describing charts or graphs by writing about these visual aids.
- Read + write learners also enjoy word games, writing in journals, reading text from different resources, and learning the definitions of new words.
- These learners are very interested in words that have fascinating origins or meanings.
- During their free time, you will see these students reading books.

Simply put, read + write learners are all about learning through written words. Read + write learners are the best types of students for language and literacy teachers. Of course, you don't have to be a language or literacy teacher to engage your read + write learners in class. For read + write learners, here are some strategies for you:

- This learning style is easy to please, especially if you

focus on traditional teaching methods. You can give your read + write learners opportunities to read books, do research online, write essays, and create book reports.

- Give your students opportunities to create lists wherein they would categorize things or concepts in order.
- These students also enjoy proofreading activities where they would have to correct mistakes in written text.
- Find a good balance between giving your students reading tasks and activities that allow them to express themselves through writing.
- Encourage your students to take down notes while you are discussing. This will give them effective resources for when they need to review or reinforce what they have learned. Typically, read + write learners would write down very detailed notes which makes reviewing easier for them. This allows them to explain concepts using their own words.
- Distribute handouts and reading lists to keep your students engaged in your lessons.

Aside from using these strategies, you should also know the areas or methods that read + write learners might find challenging. These include:

- Having to give oral presentations in front of the class.
- Studying in a noisy classroom—this will make them very distracted, and they won't be able to learn.
- Collaborating with other students as they prefer working or learning on their own.
- Having to learn without using any kind of written resources.

SOCIAL LEARNERS

Social learners are the ones who respond well to social interaction. These learners typically have strong leadership skills, and they enjoy learning and working with other students. If you have social learners in your class, you can watch them bloom by giving them a lot of group activities. These learners find pleasure in collaboration, and they're very good at communicating with others. They learn while discussing and brainstorming concepts and ideas.

Social learners are also generally good at listening. They are both understanding and thoughtful. If you have social learners in class, you will see them perform at their best when they have the chance to work with others in groups. Here are some other characteristics of social learners to look out for, so that you can identify them in your class:

- Social learners are extroverts.
- Social learners love bouncing their ideas off other

people which is why they are very good at interacting and communicating.

- They are very good at reading facial expressions and emotions.
- Because of their nature, social learners often grow up to become social workers, psychologists, teachers, and other occupations that involve a lot of social interaction.

Simply put, social learners are all about learning through social interaction. Social learners are the best types of students for all types of teachers since they will learn effectively no matter what subject you are teaching as long as you allow them to learn with others. For social learners, here are some strategies for you:

- When teaching subjects like literature or history, have a lot of role-playing activities. Afterward, have a discussion where your students can ask questions and bounce ideas off each other.
- When assigning comprehension exercises, allow your students to work in groups then present their findings in front of the class.
- When giving your students math problems to work on, especially complex ones, allow them to collaborate in groups.
- Allow your social learners to share their topics, ideas, and concepts with you and the rest of the class.

- When you have group activities in class, give your
  social learners the opportunity to share stories with
  each other to enrich your class discussions.
- Give your social learners time to have one-on-one
  discussions with you once in a while. These can be
  very valuable learning experiences for both of you.

Aside from using these strategies, you should also know the
areas or methods that social learners might find challenging.
These include:

- Being assigned to work on a task on their own,
  especially if they're not interested in the lessons you're
  trying to teach.
- When they feel like they aren't allowed or aren't
  given the opportunity to express themselves like in
  the case of students who have very strict, traditional
  teachers.
- Feeling like they cannot approach their teachers to
  share their ideas.

It's also important to note that social learners, although highly
enthusiastic, might cause distractions in your class. This is
because social learners always feel the need to share their
thoughts out loud and socialize. If you have a lot of social
learners in your class and you want to prevent too much social-
ization, you should come up with a number of group activities

that will allow them to use their energy in productive ways like the ones mentioned above.

SOLITARY LEARNERS

Solitary learners are the ones who respond well to self-study techniques. They are the opposite of social learners, and they prefer learning on their own. Other students might consider them cold or shy since they don't interact with others much. If you notice any solitary learners in your class, you should try to make them feel more comfortable so that they will come out of their shell.

You can easily notice solitary learners as they tend to keep to themselves. When it comes to working or studying, they prefer to do these things on their own. These students have high self-awareness which means that they are very in tune with their emotions and thoughts. Here are some other characteristics of solitary learners to look out for, so that you can identify them in your class:

- Solitary learners are introverts.
- Solitary learners need to be in a quiet environment for them to focus on their work and learn effectively.
- They don't like being a part of the crowd so you can easily spot solitary learners as they would be sitting away from the other students.
- Solitary learners are very independent. If you have

students like this, it's better to allow them to process information at their own pace instead of forcing them to collaborate with others in a group.

- Students with this learning style aren't too keen on being given responsibilities that involve supervision or leadership.
- They are also very creative which is why many solitary learners typically enter creative fields when they grow up.

Simply put, solitary learners are all about learning through independence and self-study. Solitary learners are the best types of students for teachers who know how to encourage shy, introverted students. Many teachers find this type of learner to be challenging, especially if they don't participate in class. But there are things you can do to give your students the best possible learning experience. For solitary learners, here are some strategies for you:

- First, try not to feel too stressed when you discover solitary learners in your class. Usually, these learners would sit silently without participating but when assessment time comes, they might even have the highest marks in your class.
- Still, finding ways to engage them makes learning more enjoyable for them. To do this, you can provide a

lot of visual learning aids like books and other similar materials.

- Schedule "quiet time" or assign "quiet spaces" in your classroom to give your solitary learners a time or a place to think and process information without distractions. This helps them learn more effectively.

- Provide activities that involve solving problems on their own.

- When assigning activities, explain their importance. Generally, solitary learners are interested in the outcomes, therefore, knowing the significance of activities may help them feel more interested.

- It's also a good idea to give these students ways for them to keep track of their own progress. This may help them feel more motivated.

- Also, have one-on-one sessions with these students so that you can ask them about their thoughts and feelings.

- Give out study guides, especially to your solitary learners, so that they have something to refer to when they are self-studying.

Aside from using these strategies, you should also know the areas or methods that solitary learners might find challenging. These include:

- Having to give reports or presentations in front of the

whole class. Such activities might make solitary
learners feel very uncomfortable

- If you make group discussions in the class mandatory.
- Working in environments that are noisy or filled with
  distractions.

VERBAL LEARNERS

Verbal or "linguistic" learners are the ones who respond well to
using their linguistic skills for writing and communicating.
They love to learn, especially when it comes to speaking, writing, reading, and listening. Verbal learners are huge fans of
rhymes, word games, and they typically have strong public
speaking skills. If you have verbal learners in your class, you
would know them by how well they use words in their writing
and when they are giving speeches.

These learners can express themselves easily both in written
and oral form. Since they enjoy reading, verbal learners also
have a great vocabulary making them the best candidates for
debates, essay writing, and other similar competitions. Here are
some other characteristics of solitary learners to look out for so
that you can identify them in your class:

- The preferred learning method of verbal learners is
  anything that involves words. These students won't
  have any problem expressing themselves through

writing or speaking because words are their main interest.

- If you notice some students who have excellent memory skills, they are probably verbal learners.
- Because of their characteristics and love of learning, many verbal learners grow up to become professors, teachers and have other professions in the field of education.

Simply put, verbal learners are all about learning through words. Verbal learners are the best types of students for literacy, language, and English teachers. Of course, since all subjects involve written and spoken words, they may excel in other subjects too. For verbal learners, here are some strategies for you:

- When it comes to verbal learners, some are more adept at reading and writing, while others are more adept at listening and speaking. If you have verbal learners in class, you should try to find out what type of verbal learners they are.
- If you want to keep your verbal learners engaged, create outlines or handouts for your lessons or presentations. Then hand these written documents out before class starts to give them a guide to follow.
- Include plenty of writing activities in your lesson plans.

- Also, include plenty of presentations or discussions. This gives your students a chance to express themselves verbally in front of the rest of the class.
- One fun activity you may want to try with these learners is to give them a script or some other reading material for them to read out loud. Then encourage them to read using different tones, voices and expressions to make things more fun and interesting.
- Encourage these learners to jot down notes while listening. After the class, you can even ask them to summarize the lesson in front of the class using the notes they wrote down as their reference.
- Since verbal learners are all about words, you can use a combination of techniques to help them learn. For instance, you will write things on the board while discussing, to hone their reading skills. After that, you give them a chance to create an outline of the lessons they have learned to hone their writing skills. Asking your students to read their outlines aloud hones their speaking skills while listening to the other students present their outlines or summaries hones their listening skills. In a single class, you can incorporate different activities that will engage your verbal learners from start to finish.

Aside from using these strategies, you should also know the areas or methods that verbal learners might find challenging. These include:

- When they have to learn by trying to understand information that is presented in an abstract way. For instance, when learning math, these learners would prefer word problems to problems that involve formulas and equations.
- Having to perform activities that require visual-spatial skills or hand-eye coordination.
- Trying to interpret information presented in a visual way like reading maps, graphs or charts.

VISUAL LEARNERS

Visual learners are the ones who respond well to the use of visual aids like images, diagrams, colors, pictures, and film clips. They are very good at interpreting or describing information presented visually like in the cases of graphs, charts, and maps. If you have visual learners in class, you will notice that they learn through observation. When you are explaining something and you use visual aids, these learners would be focused on you intently.

Using a lot of visual aids while teaching is the best way to engage your visual learners. Since they are very good at visualizing information, they typically have a great sense of direction too. Most visual learners are also fond of scribbling, drawing, and doodling. Here are some other characteristics of visual learners to look out for so that you can identify them in your class:

- Visual learners prefer to learn through observation and sight. If you hear your students say things like, "let me see that" or "can you show me?" they are probably visual learners.
- You know that a student is a visual learner if they learn how to accomplish a task after watching you do the task or after seeing visual instructions like illustrations or images that show how the task is done.
- Because of the nature of their interests, many visual learners end up in industries that involve design, art, photography, and even architecture when they grow up.

Simply put, visual learners are all about learning through the use of visual aids. Visual learners are the best types of students for art teachers. Of course, you don't have to be an art teacher to engage your visual learners in class. For visual learners, here are some strategies for you:

- Engage your visual learners by including a lot of imagery in your presentations. Find ways to incorporate these elements without straying from the concepts or lessons you plan to teach. For instance, if you're teaching math, use diagrams. If you're teaching history or geography, using maps will keep these learners engaged.

- Use visual cues and color-coding if applicable to your lessons. These can help your students visualize information in a more organized way.
- If you can't find ways to use visual aids in your presentations, use visual metaphors and analogies instead. This may help your students visualize the concepts on their own.
- Give your students opportunities to create their own drawings, charts, diagrams, and even mind maps as part of the reinforcement exercises after you have taught a new lesson.
- Have storytelling activities often. This is especially beneficial for younger students. It's easy to add images to stories which means that this activity will definitely engage your visual learners.
- If you give handouts that only consist of text, allow your students to highlight the most important points using different colors of highlighters. This makes the handout more interesting for them even though it doesn't contain any visual elements.
- Use fun visual aids like flashcards, caricatures, and pictures when reviewing concepts in the class.

- When arranging your students in class, you may want to put your visual learners at the front of the class.

Aside from using these strategies, you should also know the areas or methods that visual listeners might find challenging. These include:

- Sitting through discussions, lectures or lessons that don't involve any kind of visual elements.
- Working in a classroom where there is too much noise or other kinds of distractions.
- Listening to oral instructions then having to figure out what those instructions mean.
- Having to sound out words without any pictures to guide them.

2

FINDING THE PERFECT BALANCE

Have you ever heard of blended learning?

This is an innovative approach to teaching that combines traditional methods with online educational opportunities, and materials. This approach is relatively new as teachers all over the world are now looking for ways to reach out to their students no matter what the situation is. For instance, in the time this book was written, we are faced with a global pandemic due to the infamous COVID-19. Because of this pandemic, parents feel apprehensive in terms of sending their kids to school since this disease gets transmitted easily.

This is a very real situation that serves as an important example of how blended learning helps students all over the world continue with their education despite the situation. While students have to learn from home, teachers like you and me can continue educating students through online learning methods. Of course, even if the world goes back to "normal" and both teachers and students can start attending school, blended learning can still be highly beneficial.

Although this method is fairly new, it is modern and it fits in well with our modern lifestyle. Since most students spend a lot of time in front of computers and other electronic devices, learning through these things is a lot easier for them. As a teacher, blended learning is something that you should learn. Even if you are more comfortable with traditional learning styles, you might be surprised at how effective this approach will be to your life as a teacher.

In this chapter, you will discover the benefits of a blended learning environment. You will learn what it entails and how you can apply blended learning to your classroom whether you are teaching online courses or you have been teaching using traditional methods ever since you became a teacher.

THE BEAUTY OF BLENDED LEARNING

Blended learning is a type of teaching style or approach that combines traditional teaching methods with more modern online educational materials and methods to help make learning a more holistic experience for different types of learners. Blended learning can mean different things. But the most basic definition of this approach means that you as a teacher would physically teach your students in class while using a combination of traditional and contemporary methods.

But it can also be the other way around. If you are a teacher of an online class, you can also employ traditional methods of teaching to make your classes more interesting. Either way, this approach must include different methods for you to cater to the educational needs of your students. As a teacher, you have complete control over the time, place, and pace of your lessons. You would also be in charge of the methods you use to teach your students which is why blended learning can also make teaching significantly easier for you.

Today, we rely heavily on digital devices and this is one of the main reasons why blended learning emerged as a modern approach to teaching. This contemporary teaching style enables you to maximize the educational impact of learning for your students because you would be using the methods that have been tried-and-tested for years, while employing online methods that are typically more appealing to modern-day students. Essentially, blended learning allows you to break free of the traditional methods without forgetting them entirely. These days, blended learning is becoming increasingly popular because of the many benefits it has to offer.

BENEFITS FOR TEACHERS

As a teacher, you should already be familiar with the traditional teaching methods. We have all tried teaching in a classroom and if you have been teaching for some months now, you would already feel comfortable in front of the class. If blended learning is new to you, then you can see it as an opportunity to challenge yourself to become a better teacher. Take a look at the benefits this teaching approach has to offer for you as a teacher:

- Since there are so many online resources you can use right now, you can easily save time on lesson planning by making modifications to the online resources you use if you need to teach different classes. For instance, if you have a math class and a science class, you can have the same flow for both classes but use different online resources.
- You can empower your students and keep them motivated by assigning them to do online activities while you guide or supervise them. As long as you learn how to conduct these activities, teaching becomes much simpler for you.
- Students these days are very interested in online activities which makes it easier for you to keep them engaged.
- It's easier for you to keep track of your students' progress using online reports and lesson statistics, for

example. By using these tools, you can gain valuable insights into the learning rates of your students.

- Giving online activities means that you won't have to print out worksheets or examinations on paper. This makes blended learning, particularly the digital side, more sustainable and environmentally friendly.
- By using online systems, checking and grading activities becomes automated. This saves you a lot of time and effort.
- It allows you to be more flexible in class. As you plan your lessons, you can include both methods and see what your students are interested in for the day. By having these choices, you can give your students the freedom to help you decide how your lesson goes. This is an amazing way to keep your students motivated throughout the day.

The bottom line is that blended learning gives you greater control over how you help your students learn. Since you will have access to both the traditional methods and the more modern ones, you can follow the learning pace of your students while still working towards your goals as a teacher.

BENEFITS FOR STUDENTS

The great thing about blended learning is that the benefits aren't one-sided. As a teacher, blended learning makes things easier for you. But for students, this teaching style also offers a number of excellent benefits:

- Blended learning allows students to support each other while learning. This peer support is established through communication both online and offline. While your students meet each other in the classroom every day, they can still continue working and communicating with each other to discuss lessons or projects even when they are not in school.
- Whenever you introduce new concepts or reinforce old concepts in class, your students can easily access online resources to help them learn. If you provide them with such resources, learning becomes much more interesting and easier for your students.
- Just as blended learning makes you a more flexible teacher, this teaching approach allows your students to learn in a more flexible way too. They have the option to learn through books, class discussions, and other traditional methods while also having access to online resources that are much more interesting for a lot of students these days. In other words, blended learning gives students more freedom to learn according to their preferred methods.
- When students are allowed to learn based on their preferred learning methods, this enhances their retention. For instance, if you introduce online games

that reinforce the concepts you learned in class, this fun way of learning may help your students remember the concepts easier.

- Blended learning improves your students' relationship with technological devices and the online world. Instead of just using these modern conveniences to play games or spend their time doing irrelevant things, your students will use them for learning.

- By introducing your students to an online learning space, you are also preparing them for the future. The combination of online and traditional learning hones their soft skills such as critical thinking, team cooperation, time management, and even their ability to communicate and relate more effectively with others.

Through blended learning, you will notice an increase in your students' learning in terms of effectiveness and satisfaction. These days, teachers need to find ways to inspire and motivate students. To become the best teacher for your students, learning how to apply blended learning is key. This approach fosters creativity, it keeps your students interested, and it even promotes self-learning. As you give your students the freedom to reinforce what they have learned outside of the classroom, they will feel more motivated to pursue further learning on their own.

Blended learning is part of our present and future as teachers. It has transformative power as it matches the current needs, interests, and lifestyle of our modern-day students. Now that you know the advantages of this revolutionary teaching approach, here are a few practical tips for you to apply. These will give you a better idea of how you can start using the blended learning approach in your classroom:

Incorporate online lessons and resources when planning your class syllabus and daily lessons

For you to start practicing blended learning, the first step is to incorporate these methods into your plans. This is especially important if this is your first time using online methods, materials, and activities. By including these modern additions in your plans, you can plan your schedule more effectively. Also, planning forces you to familiarize yourself with the different online resources available. After all, you can't include online activities in your plans if you don't know what kind of online activities are available, right?

Find out what resources you have and what you have to acquire

In line with the first point, you should take the time to assess how much you know in terms of online methods—and what you need to learn. For instance, you watch a lot of videos online to help you learn new teaching methods. You can use your skill of finding great videos for learning to find equally amazing videos to help your students understand their lessons better. But if you have no idea what online resources offer the best, high-quality learning materials and activities, this is something you have to work on. Usually, you can learn this by doing research.

Keep changing and improving your methods until you find the perfect balance

As you start combining traditional methods with online ones, you should also observe how these combinations are working for your class. Do you notice an improvement in your students' motivation or are the online activities making them feel confused? If you see improvements, keep going. But if you see that the methods you have chosen aren't working, you need to make some adjustments or modifications to your plan. Keep observing your students as you start practicing blended learning so that you will know what's working and what isn't.

When it comes to blended learning, the best way to incorporate this teaching approach is by trying it yourself! It might seem radically different, especially if you have zero experience with online methods but in the long-run, you will make things better for yourself and your students. This flexible approach is a lot of fun once you get the hang of it. But you will only learn how to use blended learning by applying it in your classroom.

TRIED AND TESTED TRADITIONAL LEARNING TECHNIQUES

Although blended learning is both effective and popular, it's important to remember that half of this learning approach is traditional learning. Online courses might be very popular these days but there is nothing like the tried-and-tested traditional classroom methods. As a teacher, these methods will always be part of your life. And in some cases, traditional learning methods are the most effective.

Traditional learning classes are suitable for students of all ages. As your students come into the classroom each day to learn, you get to know them—and they get to know you—better. Here are the standout benefits traditional learning methods have to offer:

More effective learning because of the human element

By far, this is the most important benefit of traditional learning. Employing traditional methods will always involve you. When it comes to online learning, you can take a step back and allow your students to learn and discover things on their own. In most cases, your main purpose would be to facilitate their learning. But for traditional methods, you play an active role in your students' learning.

It promotes active learning

Traditional learning means that your students will participate in the class as you are teaching them. This real-time interaction helps promote active learning, especially if you find ways to engage the different types of learning in your class. By using the traditional learning methods, you will give your students a chance to listen, ask questions, and even share their ideas in class. This is a very important part of learning that helps increase comprehension.

Fewer distractions

While online learning can be very effective, it can also be a huge distraction. Instead of self-studying or accomplishing the online activities you have assigned, your students might use their time browsing websites, reading articles or exploring social media platforms that have nothing to do with your lessons. These distractions are extremely tempting and once your students give in to them, they will end up wasting a lot of time. But when you use traditional learning methods, you don't have to worry about these distractions as your students will be focused on you and the activities you give them in the class.

The opportunity to offer extracurricular activities

Traditional methods allow you to offer more enriching activities to your students such as field trips, clubs, sports, and other school activities. These real-life experiences are unique to traditional learning methods as you cannot apply them to online learning. These activities are very important as they teach life lessons that students cannot learn as effectively through online methods.

It promotes group interaction

This is a clear advantage of traditional learning methods. Although students can communicate with each other online as well, being able to communicate face-to-face hones your students' ability to interact with others. For instance, if you give a group activity, your students can have discussions and sharing sessions right after you have introduced a concept. This allows them to give immediate feedback to each other too. For some students, this interaction allows them to hone their leadership skills too. By learning together in one class, your students develop their interpersonal skills while feeling more engaged in the learning process.

More structured

Finally, traditional learning offers a better structure and organization. You can create a schedule for your class to follow then assign specific times to the activities you have planned. This trains your students to become disciplined, punctual, and to learn how to use their time in the most productive way possible. It also teaches accountability to your students as they learn how to follow the schedule you have set for them.

As you can see, traditional learning is truly beneficial. Although they might seem "old-fashioned," these learning methods still work. Now, if you want to combine these methods with modern activities, here are some pointers for you to start with:

- Start by making a list of your most effective traditional methods. Then create another list wherein you include all of the online resources that you may use in combination with those methods.

- Assess your teaching methods to find out what works effectively and what you need to improve. You might discover that some of your traditional methods work better when you reinforce them with online activities. Or you might see how some of your methods can be replaced with modern, digital options that will help your students learn better.

- Once in a while, try to flip your methods to see if this sparks your students' interests. For instance, at the beginning of your class, allow them to watch a video to introduce the concept then continue by employing traditional methods to explain the concept further.

- You may consider using online assessment tools. Although written assessments are the traditional way to go, digital options might be easier for you, and they might save you a lot of time.

- If you give assignments to your students, allow them to use online resources to help them out. This might make your students more motivated to accomplish the tasks you assign to them.

- Give your students the option to complete individual or group activities either in your classroom or online. Before assigning an activity, ask them whether they would like to complete it in class together, or they would like to communicate online to work on the activity after class.

Blended learning is all about finding ways to combine different methods to give your students opportunities to grow and excel. Now that you have a better idea of how you can use traditional methods in blended learning, let's move on to the other half of the equation.

NEW AND INNOVATIVE DIGITAL LEARNING TECHNIQUES

Even though new and innovative methods are emerging in the world of education, you should not set aside the tried-and-tested traditional methods that teachers all over the world have been using for years. Instead, you should focus on combining these "old-fashioned" methods with contemporary methods to improve the learning experiences of your students. As a teacher, you can employ the use of online learning tools in your physical classroom to make things better for everyone. This is where your teaching style will become more interesting as you learn all about the different strategies for blended learning.

While blended learning may involve online learning methods, these are two different things. Online learning mainly involves students taking online courses or classes. Unfortunately, this isn't ideal for students of all ages, especially young children as they tend to have shorter attention spans. Blended learning, on the other hand, is all about finding ways to incorporate online tools and methods. Here are some examples:

Using a learning management system

A learning management system is a type of software application that you can use to deliver, document, monitor, report, and automate training programs, development programs, learning programs or educational courses. This is a concept that came about after e-Learning gained popularity.

You can use an LMS to deliver lessons, create reports, monitor the progress of your students, and more. The things that you can do with an LMS depends on the software that you choose. A simple online search using the keywords "learning management system" or "LMS" will already give you a number of options to choose from. Before you download or purchase software to use in your class as part of your blended learning approach, make sure to learn all about them first. This allows you to choose the best LMS to suit your needs and preferences.

Hosting webinars or online classes once in a while

As you introduce blended learning to your students, you can host online classes or webinars so that your students can continue learning in the comfort of their homes. These are great options for when you cannot go to school or if you just want to shake things up to keep your students interested.

To host webinars and classes online, you need the right tools. These days, the most popular tools are Zoom, Google Hangouts, and Adobe Connect. After choosing which tool to use, encourage your students to download the same tool. Also, make sure that you teach your students how to use the tool so that they can join your webinars without issue.

These are two of the best examples of how you can combine your traditional teaching methods with online tools and methods. Now, if you combine these two together for your blended learning approach, this allows you to:

- Organize your lessons more effectively while avoiding task repetition.
- Schedule classes in your chosen LMS and sync this with your webinar tool for easier scheduling.
- Register your students using the LMS so that their registration details automatically go to your webinar tool.

The great thing about online tools is that you can usually link or sync them so that they work together automatically. That way, you don't have to update each of these tools separately as this will take a lot of time and effort. Generally, the main purpose of adding online tools to your teaching methods is to simplify your processes to make you more productive overall.

As more teachers have started adapting the blended learning approach, various models have emerged. By choosing one of these models, you might find it easier to adjust to the unique teaching style. The model that you choose depends on the needs of your students and the direction that you want to take in your classroom. To give you an idea of how to incorporate one of the blended learning models in your class, let's take a look at some of the most basic ones that are easiest to apply in class:

ROTATION MODEL

The Rotation Model involves helping your students learn a specific academic course or subject by rotating their learning environments. Since this is a variation of the blended learning approach, it means that you will rotate between traditional, face-to-face lessons, one-on-one sessions with your students, online classes with assessments, written assignments that you assign to your students at home, and group discussions. This model is quite effective, especially for older students who don't rely on routines and consistency.

Here are some benefits to expect from the Rotation Model:

- You can use this model no matter how big or how small your class is.

- It allows you to help a large class of students learn more effectively.
- When breaking your class down into smaller groups or having one-on-one sessions, you can learn more about your students and the subjects or concepts where they need more guidance.
- You can use an LMS to keep track of your students' attendance and progress every time they attend online classes or take online assessments.
- It allows you to teach different lessons and concepts simultaneously as you work with different groups within your class.
- You may notice an increase in student engagement and motivation as they feel challenged by the rotation in their learning environments.

Effective as this model is, it does come with its own downsides including:

- It takes a lot of time and effort to plan all of the learning environments for your students.
- You need to have the experience (and confidence) to create assignments and activities for small groups of learners.
- If you have no experience with online methods and activities, it might be challenging for you to think of

several activities to engage your students simultaneously.

- You should first make sure that all of the online activities you provide are well-built and well-tested so that your students can accomplish them without supervision.
- Since only half of your reports and activities will be online, you have to come up with a system to collate all of your data.

Simply put, this model can be extremely fun and beneficial for your students but you should already have an idea of how you will execute it. Before introducing this model to your students, you have to do a lot of research and planning first.

ONLINE LAB MODEL

The Online Lab Model allows you to work with your students at their own pace, however, it's not suitable for all schools. For instance, if your school doesn't have enough computers to accommodate all of your students, then this model might not be feasible. Here, the learning is mostly done online and your traditional methods would only be used on occasion. Therefore, you would mainly be facilitating the activities of your students.

Although students may find this model appealing, not all teachers would appreciate it. After all, it doesn't incorporate the traditional methods that most teachers are comfortable with.

Also, if your students transfer to a new school, they might find it challenging to cope with the traditional learning methods. If you really want to go through with this model that focuses mainly on online learning, try to find the right balance to make it more effective and realistic.

SOCIAL MEDIA BLENDING MODEL

The Social Media Blending Model allows you to integrate social media into your classroom—something that many of your students will appreciate. As you integrate social media into your students' learning processes, you will allow them to use the common tools used in these platforms. While learning basic concepts, you can also encourage your students to learn modern skills like blogging, video conferencing, and creating online content, for example.

Your students can interact with each other inside and outside of the classroom as they have online discussions no matter where they are. While this model is innovative and exciting, it becomes easier for you to set aside the traditional techniques. To ensure that you are still using the blended learning approach, come up with interesting and engaging classroom activities to complement the social media activity you allow your students to participate in.

MOODLE MODEL

The Moodle Model involves using "Moodle," which is an open-source learning management system that you can use together with your traditional learning methods. Through Moodle, you can post videos, lectures, assignments, and other learning resources for your students to see. By downloading this software, your students can interact with you and their classmates in chat rooms, discussion forums, and by sending private messages. You can even use this to record the results of your students' assessments both online and offline. This is an excellent tool to use in combination with face-to-face classes.

Blended learning becomes much easier for you when you choose one of these models or come up with your own plan for how to combine traditional and contemporary methods. Now that you have learned all about traditional and online methods, it's time to put them together so that you can start giving your students the blended learning experience. Here are some tips for you to do this:

Come up with a plan

Before integrating new methods into your classroom, come up with a plan first. Make a list of all the methods—traditional and online—that you want to use. After this, take time to reflect and think about which methods will work in your class and which ones won't. For instance, if you want to have group discussions in class because you have a lot of social learners, having a lot of online group activities might be too redundant. Remember, you want to complement your traditional and online methods to create a more engaging learning experience for your students. To do this, you have to plan things carefully.

Use what you have

If this is the first time for you to use blended learning, you don't have to change everything! In fact, you may already have amazing lesson plans and your own unique teaching style to start with. Now, all you have to do is think of ways to add online methods, tools, and activities to what you have now. This is the beauty of blended learning—it allows you to customize your teaching approach to make it easier for you and your students. Go back to the list you have made and try to see which online methods fit into your current teaching style and to the activities that you have tested and proven through the years.

Be there for your students both online and offline

Another great thing about blended learning is that you can be there for your students whenever they need you and no matter where you are. While in class, your students can talk to you face-to-face. But whenever they are away from school, the online platforms that you use for your lessons allow your students to reach out to you as needed too.

For instance, if you have given them homework and one of your students doesn't understand the task, they can send you a message to ask questions. Of course, you can always set guidelines for your students so that you don't have to deal with such queries all throughout the day. You can set "virtual office hours" wherein your students can expect a response from you as long as they send a message within those hours.

To get instant feedback, consider switching to digital assessments

One of the best features of online learning is giving digital assessments. Through these assessments, you can immediately get the results. If you learn how to make and give online assessments, you can say goodbye to giving written exams that take a lot of time to make, check, recheck, and grade. Doing all of this online streamlines the process giving you time to do more important things.

Mix things up!

Blended learning is all about combining methods to keep your students engaged in your lessons. Therefore, you should think of different ways to do this. Here are some examples:

- Think of group projects that involve planning in the classroom but using multimedia tools to present their final work.
- Allow your students to use their cellphones in class—as long as you have instructed them to download an app that they can use for learning. This works well if you have chosen to use the Social Media Blending Model.

- Organize study sessions both in your classroom and online. This keeps your students on their feet as they will experience different learning environments while working with each other.

When sending homework, make sure it's interesting

Homework is part of the learning process. At some point, you will assign work for your students to do at home. Although they will be accomplishing these tasks at home, you should still make the tasks interesting and engaging. This is important so that there is consistency in their learning. When it comes to homework, you can use both traditional and online methods too.

Blended learning is meant to make things fun, interesting, and easy. While learning how to incorporate different methods into your teaching style may be challenging at the beginning, you will find how incredibly easy it is once you get the hang of things. Just keep an open mind and continue observing your students to see whether your methods are working or you need to make some changes to improve your students' learning experiences.

3

LEARNING ALL ABOUT EFFECTIVE CLASSROOM MANAGEMENT

Understanding your learners and using blended learning in your classroom will put you on the path to becoming an amazing teacher—but there is still more to learn. One of the most important skills you must learn as a teacher is effective classroom management. To maximize your students' learning potential, you must discover how you manage your classroom to create a high-learning environment that's fun for your students while you still maintain authority over them.

Classroom management may seem like a simple concept, but the fact is, it involves so many things. It consists of attitudes and techniques through which you would control your students' learning environment to ensure learning. One of the most important—and challenging—aspects of classroom management is to learn how to minimize disruptive behaviors of students by redirecting their energy into something more productive. To manage your classroom effectively, you must learn how to prevent disruptive behavior. If you can't do this, the next best thing is to learn how to respond to such behavior in the most appropriate ways.

As you learn effective classroom management, you should focus on your goals and the actions you must take to reach those goals. At the end of the day, you want to create an ideal classroom environment where your students can learn without distractions. In doing this, you will feel more confident in the learning experiences that your students will have each day.

This chapter is all about classroom management. From learning what a disruptive classroom looks like to discovering how you can turn things around, there is much for you to explore if you want to become a master at classroom management.

WHAT DOES A DISRUPTIVE CLASSROOM LOOK LIKE?

In a perfect world, you will be standing in front of a quiet, well-organized group of students. The whole class would be sitting down, focused on you, and listening intently. With such a class, teaching would be a breeze.

Of course, this is rarely the case.

Often, you will get a class with a number of disruptive students who make teaching a huge challenge. On bad days, all of your students would be chatting with each other, papers would be flying around, and none of them would be listening to you. As you scream and shout to get their attention, none of them even looks at you—so you end up feeling stressed and frustrated.

Trying to teach in a disruptive class isn't ideal as this kind of environment hinders the learning curve. Furthermore, it has a negative effect on you as a teacher, as well as your students. A disruptive class is typically caused by students who display disruptive behavior. There are several factors that cause such behavior including:

Disengagement

When the lessons you teach are either too difficult or too easy for your students, they might not want to participate in class. They either feel too challenged or not challenged enough that they end up exhibiting disruptive behaviors.

Environment

When your students don't feel comfortable in the classroom, they may lash out by causing disruptions. To avoid this, you should make sure that your classroom isn't too hot, too cold or too stuffy. Also, make sure that your students aren't distracted by noises and other things that might cause them to find something better to do instead of paying attention to you.

Other factors

The other factors that might be causing disruptions in your

class are language barriers, cultural differences, the size or composition of the students in your class, and if you're trying to meet the needs of all your students separately. This might cause you to lose focus as you scramble to try pleasing everyone instead of trying to deliver your lessons to meet your goals.

In some cases, factors like the students' home environments can play a role in their behaviors at school. If some students are having issues at home, they might act out in school as a result. This is one of the most common examples of how disruptive behaviors can also originate from outside of school.

If some of your students make jokes in class once in a while, do you consider them disruptive? If the learning in your class doesn't get interrupted, then you don't have to take action against these students. However, there are certain behaviors that you must try to avoid or deal with when they happen. These behaviors are:

Abusive or derogatory language or actions

When students use abusive, derogatory, or threatening behaviors or language in class, you should intervene right away. These aren't acceptable. Speak with the parents of your students first then take the issue to your school's principal. If these steps don't work, you might have to raise the issue with law enforcement to avoid things from getting out of hand.

Excessive talking and noise-making

Students who talk too much or make a lot of noises in class cause disruptions to others. These actions make it difficult for you to teach and it makes it extremely difficult for the other students to learn. If you notice such behaviors, then it's time for you to take action. You shouldn't allow these students to dominate your classroom, otherwise, you might end up feeling frustrated every single day.

Doing unrelated activities

Although note-passing seems like a thing of the past, students these days can sometimes cause disruptions by doing things in the class that aren't related to your lessons or activities. Such behaviors include texting, playing games on their phones, eating or even sleeping in class. Naturally, when other students see some of their classmates doing these things, they get distracted.

Tardiness

Whenever you have students who always come in late, your class gets disrupted too. When a tardy student comes in, everyone's attention—including yours—goes to that student. Then you have to wait until the student settles down before you continue. In some cases, the student might even cause more disruptions by asking questions or clarifications about the lesson that you have already explained.

These are some of the most common examples of disruptive behaviors in the class. There are many more. The point is that such behaviors are a normal part of your life as a teacher. If you want to become an effective teacher, learning how to handle disruptive students is an important part of classroom management. To help you out, here are some tips:

- To avoid disruptive behaviors, set clear rules and expectations from the start. If you think it will help, write these rules down and post them somewhere in your classroom. This will remind your students of the rules you have set, so they won't have a reason to say that they forgot or that you didn't set such rules.
- Try to determine whether you have to take a break from your lecture to deal with the behavior or not. In some cases, the behaviors aren't disruptive enough that you should put a stop to them right away. In such a case, make sure to call the attention of the student causing the disruption when the rest of the class is busy with an activity you assigned. Then you can talk to the student without making them feel embarrassed in front of everyone else.
- Try to be more flexible while teaching. If the disruptions are causing everyone to be distracted, then you may have to change your teaching strategies or the lessons you have planned for the day.
- As much as possible, try to avoid losing your cool. Shouting at a student who is causing disruptions in class is never a good idea, especially for young children.

Instead, talk to the student calmly and with respect. Of course, this depends on the age of your student and their level of comprehension.

- In cases where disruptive behavior turns dangerous, ask another student to call the principal. Remain calm and distract the student until someone comes to assist you. As a teacher, you must make sure that the rest of the class is safe, therefore, asking for help is the best solution.

Disruptive behaviors don't have to ruin your teaching style or your students' learning experiences. Instead, you should learn how to communicate with your students, spot disruptive behaviors and their triggers, and deal with such behavior in the most appropriate ways.

WHY SHOULD YOU LEARN CLASSROOM MANAGEMENT?

As a teacher, you want to awaken a love of learning within your students. This will make things easier for you, for them, and for all the other teachers who will have the pleasure of teaching your students. The most effective way to promote a life-long love of learning is through proper classroom management.

Simple as this concept might seem, it is one of the biggest struggles that teachers have. Sadly, classroom management isn't something that you can learn in school. Instead, it is something you can learn through your experiences in the classroom. While you may learn a lot from classroom management tips and strategies, you still have to apply these and see what works for you and your class—and what doesn't. Through classroom management, you will be able to create a more positive learning environment for your students.

If you want to become an effective teacher, you need to learn and master classroom management. You must learn how to apply consistent and strong management skills so that you won't have to deal with common issues like disruptive behavior. Studies have shown that being confident in your classroom management skills helps with your overall emotional health and well-being. After all, if you know that you can handle your class and your students even if problems arise, you won't feel stressed when problems come your way.

When most people hear the term "classroom management," they immediately associate this with discipline or punishment. Although discipline is an important aspect of classroom management, there is more to it than that. Through classroom management, you will create an ideal environment that will be beneficial for you and your students. You do this by setting rules and expectations, using the right strategies, and by communicating openly with your students. Effective classroom management enables you to pave the way to your students' engagement in learning. But before we move on to effective classroom management tips, let's go through some of the most important reasons why you should learn classroom management:

To Improve Your Teaching

As you try to teach in a disorganized classroom where you haven't set any expectations or rules, you will realize how difficult it is to teach properly. Your students wouldn't have any idea of how to act in class, so they might think that "anything goes." This is a very dangerous mindset as it may lead to a disruptive classroom. While you try to handle these disruptive situations, you will constantly try to handle behavioral issues or redirect your students. In doing this, you lose a lot of teaching time—which is never good.

But if you are good at classroom management, you can create a well-organized classroom environment that's conducive to learning and teaching. By setting rules, your students will know what is expected of them while inside the class. For instance, if you are discussing in front of the class, your students would know that they should sit still, be quiet, and pay attention. Through classroom management, teaching becomes easier for you, and learning becomes easier for your students.

To Boost Your Morale

If you feel confident in your classroom management skills, this gives your morale a boost. Applying the right strategies and seeing good results makes you feel like a master teacher. You will see that you're bringing out the best in your students while you feel both motivated and satisfied to do your job. For instance, if you can teach one whole week without any major disruptions, this will definitely make you feel good.

On the other hand, if you teach a class wherein your students are constantly misbehaving and there are frequent disruptions, it won't be long until you feel burnt-out. This is why classroom management is essential. It helps you learn how to deal with your students in the best possible ways so that you can feel confident enough to keep going.

To Use Your Time Efficiently

Although learning classroom management takes time, it will help you use your time efficiently in the long-run. At the beginning of the school year, you will set rules, routines, regulations, and procedures for your students to follow. Your students need to learn these things before you can start seeing results. But once they have learned the routines you set, managing the class becomes a lot easier.

At some point, you will realize that you don't have to keep reminding them of the class rules and routines. When this happens, you can start using the extra time to do more productive things like having more activities or explaining concepts further, for example. At the end of the day, your classroom management skills help you become more efficient at time management too.

To Maintain Consistency

When you have solid classroom management skills, this allows you to provide your students with consistency. Each day, your students know what to expect in terms of the classroom schedule and routine. Even if you mix things up once in a while, you can still maintain consistency by making sure that your students still continue following the rules to avoid disruptions.

Even if you have to take leave from your class, you won't have to worry about the substitute teacher because you know that your students already have an idea of what they need to do. For instance, if you allow them to work on their textbooks during the first fifteen minutes of class while you wait for everyone to arrive, then they would already know what to do even when you're not around. Consistency might seem beneficial for you but it's also a big help for your students as it helps them feel more comfortable in class.

To Create a Learning Culture

As you learn and apply the different strategies of classroom management, this helps you create a structure in your class to help you reach your teaching goals. With this structure, it also becomes easier to carry out lessons in your class. Of course, this also makes it easier for you to help your students achieve their learning goals. The structure you create through classroom management gives your students a framework to follow to ensure that you are all working towards the same goals.

To Reduce Distractions and Behavioral Issues

This is the most important benefit of classroom management and it also happens to be its primary goal. If you can manage your classroom effectively, you won't be giving your students any opportunity or time to misbehave or cause disruptions. Since you have set rules and clear expectations, your students will know the consequences of such actions. Classroom management enables you to set boundaries, it helps your students understand consequences, and it helps everyone get along better in class.

THE MOST EFFECTIVE CLASSROOM MANAGEMENT TIPS EVER!

Now that you know more about classroom management, you can understand why it's so important. However, as wonderful as classroom management is, a lot of teachers struggle with it. If you're one such teacher, you should first try to determine the reason why you cannot seem to manage your class effectively. Some of the most common reasons include:

- Not having enough knowledge or experience with classroom management.
- Not having enough resources to draw inspiration from.
- Not being able to adjust to a new environment, especially if you're a new teacher.

- Not setting rules because you are trying too hard to establish relationships with your students.
- Not being confident enough to do what's needed to learn classroom management.

If you can relate to any of these reasons, you might feel worried that you can't become a master at classroom management. But one thing you must know about classroom management is that it's a skill. This means that with enough knowledge and practice, you can learn it. Once you learn it, you can keep practicing effective classroom management to help yourself improve. But to start off, here are some simple, practical, and helpful tips for you:

Start with the basics

If this is your first time to learn classroom management, you don't have to try using elaborate or complex strategies. These might make you feel overwhelmed. Instead, start with simple steps to give you confidence. When you feel like you're ready to step out of your comfort zone, then you can try to take things up a notch.

Recognize that you're the authority figure in the class

For you to manage your classroom effectively, your students must believe in you. Before this happens, you have to believe in yourself first. Even if you haven't tried any classroom management strategies before, recognize and accept that in the classroom, you are the main authority figure. You are the person in charge. As soon as you accept this, you will realize that you have the power to make things better for yourself and your students.

Optimize your classroom

Before classes start, make sure you have optimized your classroom. It must be warm, cozy, encouraging, but not distracting. For instance, if you are a preschool teacher, your class shouldn't have too many colors or characters on the walls. Otherwise, your students will only focus on these decorations instead of listening to you. Think about the age group and level of your students to help you plan the appearance of your classroom.

When it comes to seating arrangements, you have to plan this carefully too. It's recommended to assign seats instead of allowing your students to sit wherever they want. If you opt for the latter, there is a good chance that your students will sit next to each other and start chatting as soon as your class starts. Also, assigning seating arrangements gives you a chance to group your students according to their learning styles for a more effective learning experience.

Set rules and expectations

This is one of the most important parts of classroom management. On the first day of class, after you have introduced yourself and given a chance for your students to do the same, the next thing to do is to set clear, simple, and practical rules and expectations for the class.

Depending on the age of your students, you can even ask them to help you set these rules based on your expectations. After creating those rules and routines, write them down or print them out. Then display these rules somewhere visible to serve as a reminder for your students.

Build rapport with your students

The next step is to start establishing a relationship with your students. If you want them to listen and respect you, rapport is key. You want them to see you as someone approachable and caring. At the same time, you want them to see that they cannot and should not mess with you. Kind and firm, at the same time; these are not mutually exclusive ideas.

Respect is essential for effective classroom management. But it takes time to earn that respect. Don't take things too seriously but don't be too lax either. It's all about finding the right balance that allows you to be the best teacher for your students. Get to know your students by asking them questions, getting their input, and helping them out if you see that they need it. Over time, your students will come to realize that you just want what is best for them and this will make them feel more open and communicative towards you.

Create a plan for how you will manage your class

Planning is another important part of classroom management. Aside from your lesson plans, you should also come up with a plan for how you plan to deal with your students, how you plan to give them varied learning experiences, and how you plan to deal with difficult situations when they arise. With a plan in mind, managing your class becomes much easier.

After creating a plan, the next step is to gather the resources you need. For instance, after a few days of teaching, you realize that you have a lot of visual learners in your class. Now that you know this, you can come up with a plan for how to keep them engaged in your class. Since visual learners prefer learning through visual aids, you should try to gather as many visual aids as you can. Planning forces you to be more prepared in class and this will help improve your classroom management skills.

If you notice bad or disruptive behavior, deal with it right away

This is especially true if the behavior is causing disruptions to other students or to the class as a whole. When reprimanding a student, don't do it in front of everyone else. Instead, approach the student who is misbehaving to talk to them or ask them to step out of the classroom with you. Also, avoid punishing the whole class for something that one or two students have done. This will cause a lot of bad feelings which are very counterproductive to your classroom management efforts.

Give "peer teaching" a try

If you have students who excel in class and you notice that other students look up to them, this is the perfect type of situation where you can try peer teaching. Once in a while, ask your top students to take over the class while you sit down along with the other students. In such a case, make sure to follow the rules you have set to show your students that these rules apply to everyone—even to you.

Maintain consistency in terms of enforcing your rules

If you want to become a master of classroom management, maintain consistency. Keep practicing the strategies that work like setting rules or dealing with misbehaving immediately. If you discover any strategy that doesn't work for your class or situation, scrap it and try something else. But for all the strategies and rules that make it easier to manage your class, keep practicing them until you can confidently say that you have solid classroom management skills.

When you are learning and practicing classroom management, have fun with it. Don't take yourself too seriously as these tips might seem too difficult or overwhelming for you. Remember flexibility, as well. All of these things—along with the strategies that you discover on your own—will help you learn the skill of classroom management to make you the best teacher you can be.

CREATING A FUN LEARNING ENVIRONMENT

As important as classroom management is, another way for you to improve your teaching style is by learning how to make a fun learning environment for your students. If you can do this while managing your classroom effectively, then you will be able to create the best, most conducive space for your students to learn. These days, students prefer learning environments that push their learning capacity to the limit. Such environments inspire and motivate students as they see themselves reach their potentials. While planning how to incorporate fun into your students' learning experiences, consider the following factors:

- Your teaching goals
- The learning goals you have set for your students
- The characteristics of your students
- The culture that exists in your class
- Activities that promote learning
- Assessment strategies that measure your students' learning

Once you have taken all of these into account, the next thing to do is understand your classroom better. As a teacher, how do you see your classroom? Is it simply a room where your students gather? A space where you hold lectures or lessons? If your perspective of your classroom is as simple as this, then you might not feel inspired to improve it. For most students, the classroom isn't just a room they go into each day. Instead, they see it as:

- A place where they can connect with their teacher (you) and their classmates. In some cases, they create strong connections that turn into life-long friendships.
- A place where they have unique, fun experiences that awaken a love of learning within them.
- A place where they experience a wide range of feelings, moods, and emotions. Also, a place where they can express themselves and show others who they truly are.
- A place where they share stories of their lives and hear the stories of other people's lives too.
- A place where they choose to become better because they have supportive peers and an amazing teacher (you) who makes them feel motivated and inspired.
- A place they look forward to going each day. A safe space where they feel comfortable, happy, and free.

Your classroom doesn't have to be a simple place where you teach. It has the potential to be so much more—both for you and your students. As the teacher, you can transform your class into all of these things by making some changes such as:

Decorating your classroom to make it fun and functional

This takes a lot of planning, strategizing, and observing. You can start by decorating your room in a simple way at the beginning of the school year. When classes start, try to observe your students. Then you can come up with ideas and plans for how to improve the decorations of your classroom to make it both functional and fun.

For instance, if you have a class of students who are mostly interested in social media, why not decorate your room to make it "Instagrammable?" That way, your students will find it fun to simply walk into your classroom. They can take photos and even share their own ideas on how to change the decorations every month or so. This simple gesture immediately makes the learning environment more fun and engaging.

Adapting a positive mindset

No matter how beautiful your classroom is, it won't make any kind of impact without a positive mindset to go with it. Try to be as positive as possible whenever you enter your classroom. The great thing about positivity is that it can be highly contagious. If you show your students how positivity can improve their lives, they will start adopting a positive mindset too. When this happens, teaching will soon become as easy as pie!

Find different ways to engage your students in the class

Now that you know all about blended learning, you can use both traditional and online methods to teach different concepts to your students. Gone are the days when teachers would stand in front of the classroom until the bell rang. Now, you can come up with unusual, exciting, and varied ways to keep your students engaged. Some examples are:

- Breaking your class into groups so that they can discuss the lessons together.
- Introducing games to reinforce the lessons you have taught.
- Using visual aids and materials to make things more interesting for your students.
- Engaging their senses by allowing your students to experience the concept through their sight, hearing, smell, touch, and even taste.
- Promoting movement by incorporating physical activities into your lessons whenever relevant.

Use interactive activities and lessons

This is another tip where blended learning comes in. These days, collaborative learning is all the rage. You don't have to stick with traditional methods anymore. To make things more fun, invite other instructors and teachers to come to your class or have them teach your class through an online platform. If you're interested in learning more about online learning, go ahead and purchase another book I have written that is all about online teaching. I hope that this book is helping you think of creative ways to incorporate interaction into the lessons and activities you introduce to your students. In doing this, you can even reduce disruptive behaviors because your students will be too busy having fun!

Once in a while, host parties to celebrate achievements

Instead of highlighting the achievements of only your top students, you can hold parties whenever all of the students in your class have reached a particular milestone or have achieved something together as a class. For instance, if you assigned a difficult project and all of your students completed it (regardless of the results), throw a mini-party to celebrate. Acknowledging the hard work of your students will keep them motivated. Having the chance to celebrate each other's successes will bring your students closer to you and to each other.

Make free time fun too

Free time is an essential part of your students' learning environment. Including this in your class schedule gives your students a much-needed break while still giving them an opportunity to learn in your class using their preferred methods. Even if you don't ask your students to do certain things during their free time, you can prepare the environment to encourage learning. Some ways to do this include:

- Creating a "quiet space" where students can rest, read or even complete unfinished tasks.

- Filling the shelves of your classroom with audio and picture books that are related to the lessons your students are currently learning.
- Creating a "group station" where students can collaborate, discuss or play games without causing disruptions to others.

Such activities provide your students with indirect opportunities to continue their learning even during free time. Since you won't be telling them to participate in these activities, they will feel more willing to do them. It's a win-win situation.

When it comes to creating a fun learning environment for your students, the bottom line is to create a classroom that is student-centered. While you may have your own teaching goals, doing everything you can to make learning fun for your students will help you achieve those goals. When your students realize that learning is fun, teaching becomes easier for you. And you can do this by combining these strategies you have just learned with the classroom management techniques. Come up with a plan of your own that includes these strategies then watch the magic happen in your class...but we're not done yet! There is more to learn.

4

BECOMING A TEACHER WHO MOTIVATES AND INSPIRES

B y now, you should already feel more confident after everything you have learned in the previous chapters. But there are other things that will make things better—and easier for you. After reading the title of this chapter, you might be wondering how something so abstract comes after technical concepts like classroom management and blended learning.

As a teacher, you want to learn how to be inspiring so that you can motivate your students to be the best they can be. Student motivation is something that a lot of teachers struggle with, especially at this particular time in our lives. At the time of writing this book, we are currently facing a global pandemic that has changed the various aspects of our lives—probably forever.

Teachers all over the world are trying to learn how to reach out to their students through online platforms while still being able to engage them and keep them motivated. As the first in a series of books, you will learn here how to prepare yourself for this change. After this, you can purchase the second book in the series where you learn how to create courses online—then move on to the third book in the series where you learn how to teach the courses you have created in the most effective way possible.

Since online learning has become part of the "new normal," how do you keep your students motivated? If you already struggled with student motivation in the past, learning how to motivate your students while trying to master blended learning that focuses more on the online side can be more of a challenge.

But it doesn't have to be.

In this chapter, you will learn all about student motivation. As a teacher, having to deal with an unmotivated class of students is extremely difficult. If you don't do something about it, you might lose your motivation as well. As a teacher, feeling unmotivated causes a disruptive cycle that affects the quality of your class and the educational standards of your teaching. Your lack of motivation will have a negative impact on the learning of your students along with your ability to create a fun, engaging environment for your class.

As a teacher, you should learn how to become an inspiration! Motivating your students is easy if you can inspire them from the very beginning. Since inspiration and motivation begins with you, here are a few things you may want to start off with to make you feel better about yourself and passion:

- Consider practicing motivating yourself and make you feel better before you enter your class each day.
- If you're feeling overwhelmed or burned out, talk to someone close to you. You can speak to a colleague, a close friend or a family member. Anyone who will help you get through the negativity you're feeling. This is important so you don't end up taking your frustrations out on your students.
- Seek out opportunities for professional development. Such opportunities can make you feel more confident about your skills and, when this happens, you feel more inspired too.
- If needed, take a break. Ask your supervisor for some time off so that you can relax, re-energize, and find your motivation once again.

Being an inspiration doesn't mean that you have to be happy all the time. While trying to do and be the best for your students, you must also focus on yourself. Take care of yourself to keep your motivation high. This can help you with everything else that you will learn in this chapter that's all about inspiration and motivation...

THE INSPIRING POWER OF MOTIVATION

Before you learn how to motivate your students, do you know what the word motivation means?

Motivation is a state that directs, energizes, and sustains a person's behavior. In this case, the persons you will focus on are your students. To awaken their motivation, you must come up with a set of goals and best activities that will help you—or your students—reach those goals. As a teacher, you should learn how to motivate your students. When students feel motivated, you will see the following benefits:

- Motivation directs the behaviors of your students toward specific goals.
- Motivation makes your students more persistent.
- Motivation improves your students' initiative.
- Motivation increases your students' energy levels along with the effort they put into their tasks.
- Motivation helps enhance the cognitive processing skills of your students.

In other words, motivation improves the different aspects of your students' lives in terms of learning. While motivated, students become better learners. Therefore, as a teacher, you must learn how to make learning engaging, fun, and stimulating to awaken this powerful driving force within your students.

This is especially important for students who are prone to disengagement or misbehavior. With such students, you have to double your efforts if you want to get through to them. The good news is, if you can get through to the most difficult learners in the class, it means that you would have already gotten through to everyone else. Simple as motivating your students might seem, this might not be an easy journey. In fact, it may take a lot of time and effort from you. But in the long-run, successfully finding ways to motivate your students—and keep them motivated—will benefit you and your students immensely. So your next question is...how do you motivate your students?

HOW DO YOU MOTIVATE YOUR STUDENTS?

Motivation can be a tricky thing. But as you are learning how to motivate your students, you can make things easier by observing your students carefully. The reason for this is that behaviors can be accurate indicators of motivation. By observing your students throughout the day while they are doing different things, you will get a good idea of how motivated they are. Here are some examples of behaviors to look out for while observing your students:

- The amount of effort your students put into a specific task.

- The preference your students show in certain activities over others.
- The emotions your students express while performing tasks and activities.
- The time it takes for your students to start putting their hearts into the activities or tasks that they are doing.
- The persistence (or lack of persistence) your students have towards finishing a specific task or activity.

Motivation is something that comes from within a person. It is an impulse inside a person that pushes them to accomplish an action. If students aren't motivated, then they won't act. This is why motivation is extremely important in learning. When you're learning how to motivate your students, you can focus on the two types of motivation that exist: external (or extrinsic) and internal (or intrinsic).

EXTRINSIC MOTIVATION

Extrinsic motivation is a type of motivation that occurs when a person is motivated by external factors, the most common of which are rewards and punishments. For instance, if you tell a young student to finish their work if they want to get a gold star, then they would happily do their work because they are motivated by an external reward. Of course, you can't keep doing this each time you want your students to excel in their work. Also, for older students, finding a sustainable external reward can be a challenge. Usually, older students would either get bored with the rewards you are giving or they will expect more from you.

Another example is if you punish your students who disobey you. For a student who has experienced punishment, they would feel motivated not to do the same behavior that led to being punished. But when it comes to using punishment as a motivating factor, this is usually more harmful than helpful. Punishing your students too frequently might cause them to resent you or feel scared of you, especially in the case of younger kids. Although extrinsic motivation can be a powerful thing, it's not as effective as intrinsic motivation when it comes to long-term effects.

INTRINSIC MOTIVATION

Intrinsic motivation is a type of motivation that occurs when a person is motivated by internal factors like when they do something because they enjoy it or it is important to them. If you can bring out this type of motivation in your students, then they will be able to learn more effectively. Students who are internally motivated won't need any compensation, reward or punishments to accomplish the activities or tasks that you give them. However, this type of motivation is much harder to foster.

For instance, if you have a student who is creative and enjoys creating works of art, you may see them excel in subjects like Music, Arts or even Literature. But when it's time for their Math or Science subjects, you won't see the same enthusiasm in your student because they are simply not interested in these subjects. This is where you would have to put in some extra effort to encourage intrinsic motivation. Here are some ways you can do this:

Get to know your students

If you don't know your students, you won't know how to motivate them, whether extrinsically or intrinsically. As soon as the school year starts, you should start building rapport with your students while observing each and every one of them. Over time, you will notice that some students are motivated by the same things. You will also notice that some of your students are harder to impress and motivate than others. To get such observations, you must make an effort to get to know them by asking questions, starting conversations, and watching them in class.

Help them build a solid foundation for their learning

The best way to prepare your students for their future learning is by making sure that their basic knowledge and skills are strong. For instance, if you are teaching math, start with the basics to see who is proficient and who still needs more practice. This is important no matter what skills, subjects or concepts you are teaching. That way, when you are moving forward with your lessons, your students will feel confident because they already have the skills to handle more complex tasks. This confidence can be a huge motivational booster, especially in terms of intrinsic motivation.

Give your students the freedom to choose

This is one of the best tips you can use when you're trying to foster intrinsic motivation. Since this type of motivation occurs when your students enjoy the activities they are doing, giving them a choice helps awaken their motivation. If you notice that your students are choosing a specific activity frequently, think of different ways to incorporate different concepts into that activity.

For instance, if you notice that one of your students is fascinated with matching activities, come up with matching activities for different subjects—matching flashcards with objects and numbers for math, matching objects and beginning sounds for language or even matching flags to the names of their countries! It's all about finding creative ways to get your students to reach their goals while still giving them the freedom to do the things they enjoy.

To motivate your students, you have to step back and give them a chance to grow. Once you know what makes them tick, then you can start taking action to nurture their motivation and strengthen it.

MOTIVATING YOUR STUDENTS THE RIGHT WAY

When it comes to learning, one of the biggest challenges students deal with is the lack of motivation. Even if you create an amazing lesson plan and you prepare everything perfectly, if your students aren't motivated, they won't learn. Then all of your efforts would have been for nothing. Naturally, you wouldn't want this to happen. If you have to go into a classroom filled with unmotivated students and you have to teach them every day, you will soon lose your own motivation to teach.

Motivating students can be a mammoth task but the rewards and benefits far outweigh the challenges. Besides, if you are motivated by your own passion, inspiring your students to feel motivated won't be as difficult. And when you have transformed your students into learners who are excited to participate and learn, teaching will become more enjoyable for you too. So here are some tips to enable you to foster motivation to make your teaching experience more transformative:

Start with the right attitude

The moment you enter your classroom, you should already have the right mindset, motivation, and attitude. You should have already convinced yourself that you will do what it takes to inspire and motivate your students to strive while having fun. With the right attitude, everything else will fall into place much easier.

Establish goals with your students and explain your expectations

When you set expectations and explain your reasons for these expectations, you are telling your students that you respect and believe in them. Doing this also helps your students know what they have to do in class if they want to excel. After explaining what you expect of them, take the time to establish goals with your students. Instead of setting the goals on your own and imposing them on your students, ask them to help you out. This is especially effective for older students who already know the value of goal setting.

Once in a while, offer rewards or incentives

Just because intrinsic motivation is more valuable and self-sustaining, it doesn't mean that you shouldn't try to motivate your students extrinsically. The fact is, offering rewards or incentives once in a while can help your students learn how to feel intrinsically motivated in the long-run. Just don't resort to such measures too frequently so that your students don't become dependent on them.

In line with this, you should already do away with negative motivation like punishments. Remember that punishments often lead to negative feelings towards you, the learning environment, and the whole learning process. For instance, if you constantly talk down to students who cannot seem to catch up with lessons or finish their work on time, they will learn to resent you or hate the activities that they find challenging.

Appreciate the efforts your students put into their work

For most students—even the ones who struggle—they do try to put their all into their work. As a teacher, you should learn how to appreciate their efforts no matter what the result. For instance, if you assign an activity and you know that some of your students just don't have the knack for it, don't make a big deal out of it. Express your appreciation to the whole class for trying their best even though you know that some of them don't particularly enjoy the activity.

You don't have to call each one of your students to appreciate them for their efforts. This might embarrass some students, especially if they feel self-conscious about the work they have done. Instead, just give a short statement about how proud you are of all of them because they gave their best. Simple as this gesture might seem, it can have a powerful effect on your students.

Also, you may want to start praising students for their competence, not just their natural abilities. For instance, there are some students who are naturally creative and so, they would excel in making artworks. Then there are students who will try hard to impress you even though it's clear that they don't have a real talent for art. This shouldn't matter. As long as your students genuinely tried their best, recognize them for it. This will help make your students feel more motivated even with subjects or activities that they don't excel in.

Involve your students in the learning process

Since the learning process is mainly for the students, they should be involved in it. This is why blended learning works so well. By employing different strategies, you are giving your students opportunities to show you what they can do. Aside from assigning them with activities, give them responsibilities in class too. This shows your students that you trust them. For students to learn, they should be the ones doing the work. As a teacher, your main jobs should be to guide, facilitate, and supervise. Involving your students enriches their learning while empowering them. And this helps make them feel more motivated.

Explain the relevance of your lessons by connecting them to real life

Often, students may lose their motivation to learn when they don't think that they can use the lessons they learn in the "real world." Another way to motivate them is by showing them how the lessons, concepts, and activities will all prepare them for real-life situations. While planning your lessons, always include a part where you explain or show your students the real-life application of what they learned.

For instance, if you are teaching physics to your students, try to find some experiments that you can do to show your students how the abstract concept is applicable in real-life situations. The great thing about making this connection to the real world is that when your students encounter the examples you share in class in the real world, they feel excited! They will point these things out to their parents which means that they remembered the concept and how it applies to their lives.

Focus on encouragement

Often, students look to their teachers for positive reinforcement and approval. So if you want to keep them motivated, you may want to focus on encouragement. By showing positivity, genuine care, and encouragement, your students will feel valued. As time goes by, they will start to see their own value and this is when the seed of intrinsic motivation starts to grow. When it comes to motivation, even the simplest words or gestures can go a long way.

Remember that the source and level of motivation of students are unique

Motivation is a unique thing. What motivates one student might not be as effective for another. If you find something that motivates your entire class, good for you! Most of the time though, you would have to learn what motivates each of your students so that you can take the necessary steps to help them enjoy school more.

As you learn what motivates your students, you will cultivate an amazing learning culture in your class. Focus on growth and improvement through motivation then watch your students bloom. If you can find the right balance between extrinsic and intrinsic motivation, then you can help your students become highly effective learners.

MOTIVATING STUDENTS IN THIS MODERN DAY AND AGE

Even while using blended learning techniques, you can still find ways to motivate your students. As you may already know, students these days are harder to please and even harder to motivate. Of course, that doesn't mean it's an impossible task. You have already learned a bunch of tips and techniques, now let's add a few more to your arsenal to help you become a master of motivation. Level-up your motivational skills by giving these tips a try:

When introducing assigning tasks or giving activities, make sure your instructions are very clear

Since you will be planning the tasks and activities you will give to your students, make sure that the instructions are crystal clear. If you give an activity and your students get stuck with the instructions, you can say goodbye to their motivation. This is especially important when you are introducing new tasks such as online assessments or projects that require the use of digital tools. When your students cannot understand what needs to be done, they might get frustrated. When this happens, they will lose interest in the activity no matter how interesting it would have been.

Also, make sure that the materials, tasks or activities you give are very clear and easy to understand

This tip is related to the first one. After you fine-tune the instructions, you should also make sure that the tasks, materials or activities themselves are clear, interesting, and easy to understand. Consider the level of your students. Don't give them activities that are either too easy or too challenging. If needed, make separate activities for the different learners in your class. This is an excellent way to motivate your students. As they work on the activities, they will feel confident in how well they are doing—all because you made sure that the activities suit their level perfectly.

Discover the interests of your students and use those

As you observe your students to learn what motivates them, you should also try to observe their interests. This allows you to relate your class activities and materials to what your students are interested in. For instance, if your students enjoy watching vlogs, why don't you ask them to make vlogs about the lesson they had just learned? Such an activity would be highly motivational for them and it would help reinforce your lesson too. This is also an amazing way to give your students an opportunity to express themselves creatively while learning.

Give them variety

There is nothing more demotivating than having to do the same thing over and over again. These days, standing in front of your class and explaining things the traditional way won't work anymore if that is what you plan to do every day. Instead, you should make things more interesting for your students by offering them variety. For instance, you can use different methods and materials like:

- Online games that teach academic concepts.
- Board games that involve strategic planning and thinking.
- Visual aids like videos, photos or even educational films.
- Decorations according to the season or the overall theme of your lessons.
- Group activities or projects that they can collaborate on, and accomplish together.
- A mixture of online and physical resources.

Introduce modern, cutting-edge technology

Since you want to promote blended learning, introducing new, innovative technologies can help keep your students motivated and interested. If you have the resources, you can use electronic devices like a laptop or a tablet to introduce concepts to your students. Such devices are very interesting to modern-day students because these are the things they are exposed to. You can even assign homework that involves the use of such devices so that their screen time becomes more productive.

Show your students what motivation looks like

Once in a while, have brainstorming sessions where you ask your students what makes them feel motivated. Since motivation is a relatively abstract concept, it can be a challenge to explain what it means, especially to younger kids. Instead, you can ask them questions, tell stories, and show them what it means to be motivated. This is why it's important to maintain your own motivation so that your students will see how great it is to feel motivated. This is how you become an inspiration to them.

Promote friendly competition in class

At some point, your students have to learn that there will always be others who are better than them and others who are worse. This is a reality of life that you can teach by setting a spirit of friendly competition in your class. As your students compete, lose, and win, they will feel compelled to keep trying even if they don't come out on top all the time.

Give your students opportunities to improve themselves

Aside from competitions, you can give your students other opportunities for them to improve themselves. Such opportunities can come in the form of activities, projects, and even games. For instance, if you have students who struggle with math concepts, review these through games or group work. These activities will give your students a fun way to reinforce the concepts they are struggling with so that they can improve their learning without even knowing it!

As you employ all of these tips, steps, and strategies, don't forget to keep track of your student's progress. When your students are more motivated, you should see them improve in terms of their attitude towards learning, the way they learn, and how well they understand the concepts. By keeping track of your students' progress, you will know whether the strategies you use are working or if you have to make modifications to your plans to improve them.

5

DISCOVERING THE ART OF LESSON PLANNING

Creating a lesson plan is an essential aspect of being a great teacher. Don't just think of your lesson plan as another chore to check-off on your list. Instead, you should think of it as a work of art. A lesson plan serves as your guide for what to teach to your students, the methods you will use to teach, and how you will measure your students' learning. Creating a lesson plan with clearly defined learning goals, objectives, and a metric for measuring your students' progress towards these goals will help you become more effective in the class.

A lesson plan is vital to ensuring that your students benefit as much as possible from the lessons you teach. By following your lesson plan, you can make sure that all of the time your students spend in class is productive as they learn new concepts, reinforce old ones, and they have plenty of activities that will keep them interested and engaged. In this chapter, you will learn all about the art of making lesson plans. We will discuss the different parts of a lesson plan and how to create these parts to provide the best learning experience for all of your students.

THE ART OF PLANNING LESSONS

For you to create the best lessons, you should first be aware of the types of students—or learners—you are teaching. Since we have already covered the different types of learners in the first chapter, all you have to do now is to observe your students to determine what types of learners they are. After reading the last two chapters of this book, you can always go back to Chapter 1 while analyzing your students. This will help you gain a profound understanding of how your students learn, think, feel, and function. With this information in mind, you will be ready to build your lesson plan.

Basically, a lesson plan is a step-by-step, detailed guide that contains an outline of your objectives for what you want your students to accomplish throughout the day—and how you plan to help them accomplish those goals. Building a lesson plan involves goal setting, developing lessons and activities, and deciding what materials you will use to carry out your lessons. The best lesson plans are organized, specific, and well-thought-out. No matter what level or age group of students you teach, your lesson plan must have certain components to make it effective.

Although you don't have to follow a strict format for your lesson plan (unless your school has provided one), the components you will be learning in this chapter will serve as a general guideline for you to create successful lessons for your students each day. Lesson planning is an essential part of your students' learning and your job as a teacher. Before you start planning your lessons, you must first think about the outcomes you are expecting. You need to think about this first so that you can come up with a teaching pattern that won't cause your students to deviate from the concepts or topics you want your students to learn. A lesson plan will help you and your students follow the path you need to take to reach their goals. But this isn't the only benefit of creating a lesson plan. Here are the other benefits you can look forward to:

Lesson planning makes you more organized

When you create a lesson plan regularly, you learn how to think in a more organized way. You would think about each step of your students' learning process and visualize the activities as you create your outline. When it's time to follow your lesson plan, you would teach your students to be organized as well. This is highly beneficial because a disorganized class leads to disruptions and misbehaviors. Through your lesson plan, you can balance your teaching strategies along with the lessons and activities that you teach in class. That way, you can meet all the needs of your students.

Another benefit related to this is that you will also be teaching your students how to be more organized. Your students will see that you execute your lessons flawlessly and without faltering, they will realize how important it is to create a plan. This is a very valuable life lesson that your students will benefit from too.

Lesson planning helps you feel more confident

When you are organized, you will be able to maintain control over your students and your lessons. Without disruptions, your students will be more focused in class. Teaching this kind of class will make you feel more confident. You won't have to think of ways to stop the disruptions and you won't have to think of what to do next. With a plan in place, you know what comes next—and all you have to do is execute what you have planned.

Lesson planning allows you to take a break without feeling worried

If you need to take a break for whatever reason, you won't feel worried if you have left a well-made lesson plan for the substitute teacher. You won't have to worry about what the substitute will do and if your students will learn what they need to for the day. Your substitute will also appreciate the preparation you had put into planning since they would just have to follow what you have written.

Lesson planning allows you to evaluate your lessons

This is an important benefit as it enables you to see what works and what you need to change in terms of the lessons and activities you plan for your class. By going through your lesson plan at the end of the day, you can see which activities to change, which lessons you introduced successfully, and which lessons your students need to catch up with.

A BASIC STRUCTURE PLUS LOTS OF CREATIVITY

Lesson planning is an important first step in successfully executing lessons in class. Creating a clear, concise, and well-organized lesson plan makes teaching smoother and easier for you. When creating your lesson plan, try to answer the following questions:

- What are your learning objectives and goals?
- What types of activities should you present to help your students learn the lesson effectively?
- What are the materials you need to carry out the activities?
- How do you plan to deliver your lesson?
- How will you assess your students' learning at the end of the class?

After answering these questions, you can start building your lesson plan. We will discuss the different parts of a lesson plan in detail after this, but before that, let's go through some helpful lesson planning hints for you to remember:

- Check your school's guidelines before creating your lesson plan. If there is a specific format to follow, use that format. If not, you can follow the format we will discuss here.
- If your school week starts on Monday, the best time to create your lesson plan is on Thursday or Friday. That way, you know if you need to carry over some concepts that you haven't discussed during the week.
- Consider the concepts that your students already know. You can reinforce these lessons through activities and spend more time on the concepts that they haven't learned yet.
- After thinking of the lessons you want to introduce and reinforce, the next thing to do is to think about the best way to teach your students. You can do this through discussions, activities, videos, and other blended learning techniques.
- When you are done with planning your lesson, prepare all of the materials you need for your lesson. From the materials your students need for the activities to the materials you need to teach, they should also be prepared.

- If you plan to create your lesson plan online, you can make things easier for yourself by either creating or downloading a template. Then all you have to do is input new information on the template every week.

- For printed or handwritten lesson plans, make two copies—one to keep in school and one to keep in your home. That way, you can keep going back to your lesson plans whenever you need to prepare.

- Over-plan your daily lessons. It's better to have more than enough activities than getting stuck because your students accomplished everything and you have nothing else planned. You can always carry over activities and lessons that you weren't able to discuss in the week.

- Allow for flexibility if needed. If certain situations arise that seem like perfect learning opportunities, don't be too strict on yourself. Set aside the plans you have made if there is something better or more fun for your students to do, as long as these activities will help your students reach their learning goals.

- Always end your lessons in a concrete way. This closure helps students understand the concepts better. Do this by giving a summary or a simple assessment to see how well your students have learned.

It's also a good idea to create a back-up plan in case of unforeseen situations and circumstances. Think of back-up activities too. In doing this, you will always be prepared no matter what happens in class. Now, let's go through the different parts of a lesson plan and how to create them.

OBJECTIVES, OVERVIEW, AND TIMELINE

The first part of your lesson plan should be your objectives, overview, and timeline. The objectives that you set should explain why you will be introducing a certain lesson. These objectives should also communicate what you want your students to learn from the process. They will also help you determine whether your students learned the new skills or concepts by the end of the class. Here's a tip for you: while you are writing down your objectives, create another list of questions that you will ask your students at the beginning of the lesson to get their thinking caps on.

While thinking of your objectives, you should also take into account the county or national standards, as well as, the standards of your school. Use these as your guide when thinking of and writing down objectives. While it might seem overwhelming to think of specific objectives and takeaways for your lessons, this overview is just the first step. Later on, you will break everything down to make things easier for you. So don't worry!

Remember what you want your students to learn or achieve after they have completed the lesson. In other words, the objectives of your lessons are the goals that you want your students to achieve. If you want to make focused and effective goals in your lesson plan, you may want to consider using the SMART criteria. This stands for:

- **S**pecific - Have you written down specific objectives?
- **M**easurable - Have you thought of a way to measure these objectives for you to see if your students have achieved them?
- **A**ttainable - Have you considered all of your students to ensure that they can all attain the objectives you have written down?
- **R**elevant - Have you written down objectives that are relevant to the lives of your students?
- **T**ime-based - Have you considered the timeline of your objectives to ensure that you can finish them all by the end of the class?

Consider these criteria as you create each of your objectives. Start by thinking about an action that you can relate to what you want your students to be able to learn or do after your class. For instance, if you plan to teach a new concept in class—let's say, the life cycle of a butterfly—the actions that your students must be able to do might look like this:

- **Enumerate** the different stages of the life cycle of a butterfly.

- **Explain** what happens at each stage.
- **Determine** what happens next in terms of the sequence.

If you are planning to reinforce a concept, then your objectives and the actions you think about will change. For instance, if you have already taught the concept of word problems, then the actions that your students must be able to do might look like this:

- **Perform** the correct calculations based on the word problems you have given.
- **Use** the correct formulas for their computations.
- **Create** their own word problems for the other students in the class to solve.

If you create specific goals, it becomes much easier for you to measure their learning by the end of the class. As you create your objectives, you can also start coming up with a general overview of your lesson. With this overview, you can move on to the next part of your lesson plan.

LEARNING ACTIVITIES

Now that you have your objectives and a general overview of your lessons for the week, the next things to think abou learning activities you will conduct for your students t the goals. Go through the objectives you have written down and think of the best ways to introduce or reinforce the lessons within these objectives.

When thinking about learning activities, you have to make sure that everything you come up with will be understood by your students. Think about different methods for explaining concepts so that your different types of learners will understand the concept easily. For instance, when introducing a concept like farm animals, you can tell a story, give real-life examples, allow them to watch an online video or even come up with a rhyme or a song to make things more interesting. Including different learning activities that are related to the main concepts helps your students remember what they have learned better.

With this example, you might be thinking, "How will I fit all of these activities in the given time frame?" The key here is to learn how to manage your time. This is why the first part of lesson planning includes a timeline. As you create your objectives and overview, you should already have an idea of how long it would take you to carry out those objectives. If you're teaching a simple concept, you can plan several learning activities to go with it. But if you're teaching a complex or difficult concept, you may want to break this down and spread out your objectives throughout the week. That way, you won't have to rush through the concepts just to ensure that you have covered all of the objectives. Here are a few tips for you when thinking about the learning activities in your lesson plan:

- Think about the skills your students need to acquire then think of activities that allow them to practice these skills while learning the concept. Going back to the farm animal example, you can ask your students to draw different farm animals or write down their names so that they learn the concept while practicing their fine-motor skills.
- Think about different activities that promote student engagement like group work, recitation, and activities that involve movement, for example.
- Think of learning activities that are directly related to the concept you are teaching. At the same time, try to think of learning activities that will allow you to relate the concepts to real-life situations.

While thinking of these learning activities, try to come up with an estimate for how long they will take. This might be a bit challenging at the beginning of the year. But after a couple of weeks, you will already have a better idea of how long your students need to complete certain activities. Just make sure that the activities you come up with deliver high-impact learning. These activities can come in the form of:

- **Guided learning** where you introduce a concept, give some examples, then give your students a chance to give their own input about the concept as a class.
- **Independent learning** where you introduce a

concept then give your students an activity to work on by themselves.

- **Collaborative learning** where you break your class down into groups so your students can discuss or work together on an activity with their peers.

Whatever learning activities you come up with, make sure that they are fun, interesting, and filled with opportunities for learning. Once you have these activities, the next part of your lesson plan would be super easy for you to accomplish.

MATERIALS

With your learning activities in mind, your lesson plan becomes more organized. You now have an overview of your objectives and the activities you'll conduct to help your students reach those goals. The next step is to think about and make a list of all of the materials you need for the activities. Creating a list ensures that you have everything you need to execute your lesson plan in the most effective way.

Writing down the materials you need also helps you consider how attainable your activities are. For instance, you had planned to conduct an experiment to teach a certain concept to your students. When you list all of the materials you need for the experiment, you might realize that this particular experiment requires too many materials that might not be familiar with your students. With this realization, you can decide whether to continue with the experiment on a later date after explaining the materials to your students or you can think of a simpler experiment to conduct in class.

Also, when you are writing down your materials, you can add notes on whether you need to introduce the names of the materials or how to use them first. Going back to the example of the experiment. If the experiment involves the use of an instrument that poses some level of risk—like a Bunsen burner—you may want to introduce it first along with other common instruments used for conducting experiments. One or two days before conducting the experiment, you can take some time to introduce the instruments, tools or materials along with some safety measures for handling them. By the time you introduce the experiment to your students, they would already be familiar with all of the materials you present.

Another thing to consider when writing down the materials you need for your activities is the time you need to demonstrate the use of the materials before you allow your students to do the activities on their own. Never assume that your students know how to use materials unless you have already shown them the proper way to handle these in the past. This is especially true for materials that come with an element of danger, no matter how small.

Make sure to list all of the materials you need for your activities. If needed, inform your students beforehand if they should bring materials for your activities. Some of the most common types of materials you might need for blended learning are:

- Activity kits
- A laptop or tablet for online learning
- Books
- Experiment kits
- Handouts
- Visual aids

Once you have completed the list of materials, compare it with the list of learning activities to double-check that you have written down everything you need. After this, you can move on to the next step.

DELIVERING THE LESSON

At this point, you already have your objectives, learning activities, materials, and even an estimation of the time you need for each of the activities. Now, it's time for you to think about how you will deliver the lessons to your students. For each lesson and learning activity, come up with specific steps for how you will carry them out. While composing this part of your lesson plan, try to find the answers to the following questions:

- How do you plan to introduce the topic?

- How do you plan to execute each lesson from start to finish?
- How much time do you need for each step?
- Do you need to take a break in between the steps to explain something about the lesson or activity?
- How do you include steps that promote critical thinking and problem-solving?
- How can you connect the topics or activities to real-life?

If you have planned an activity that involves the use of materials to create something—like in the case of making artworks or crafts—include the cleanup time too. While writing down the steps, don't forget to be as specific as possible. This is especially important if you plan to introduce difficult lessons or you plan to conduct complex activities. Being very specific helps you visualize all of the steps. This will also be extremely helpful if another teacher will take over your class for the day.

Although there is no standard way of conducting or delivering your lesson, you may want to follow a process. This will make it easier for you to think of the steps and how to transition from one step to another. Here is an effective process you may want to consider:

Step 1: Exploration and Introduction

First, you should introduce the topic of the day along with the learning objectives. Here's a tip for you: a fun way to introduce a topic is by having an icebreaker like a simple game or a song that involves movement. Then you can write down your objectives on the board so that you can cross them off one at a time as you progress throughout the day.

Step 2: Learning and Practicing

After introducing the concept and the objectives, it's time to start giving your learning activities. This is where you conduct all of the activities you have planned using the materials you have prepared. This part of the delivery process will take the most time. This is also where most of the learning occurs.

Step 3: Critical Thinking and Reflecting

When your students are done with their activities, take a moment to help them think about what they have learned. Here, you can ask a lot of questions (prepare a list of questions beforehand), allow them to have group discussions or give them an opportunity to write down their thoughts.

Step 4: Reviewing and Reinforcing

Finally, you can give one or two final activities that will help reinforce the learning of your students. This can be as simple as asking a few students to summarize the lesson or as elaborate as putting your students into groups and asking them to create a report about the lesson they have learned.

Simply put, this part of your lesson plan involves the most planning. Since you will think of the step-by-step progression of your lesson, you will already have an idea of how your day will go! After this, it's time to move on to the next part of your plan.

ASSESSMENT

After you have finished your procedures, you're not done yet! You still need to include the assessments. This is a crucial part of your lesson plan because you will be grading your students through their assessments. You can either include assessments at any point throughout your lesson or at the end. The type of assessment you give depends on the concept you taught, the activity you gave, and the level of learning that you want to check. Here are some examples of assessments you may give:

- Quizzes and seat work
- Writing assignments like essays, journal entries or book reports
- Hands-on activities that your students would have to complete without your guidance
- Individual or group presentations

You can even create project or lesson evaluation forms with each lesson that you teach. This is like a survey form that your students will fill out at the end of the day so that you can determine how well they have understood your lessons. You can download such a form online or create your own based on your learning objectives.

When you are thinking about the assessment method to use, remember to incorporate the objectives you have written at the beginning. At the end of the day, you want to check if your students have achieved the objectives—and you will do this through assessments. Remember that assessments don't always have to be written. For instance, if one of your objectives is for your students to learn a skill, then the assessment method you choose should allow them to practice the skill for you to check.

If your assessment isn't related to the learning objectives you have set, you wouldn't know if your students met those objectives. But if your assessments and objectives are aligned, it becomes much easier for you to make adjustments to your plans for the next days or weeks. Going back to the example of learning a skill, if you discover that your students haven't acquired the skill yet, you can make modifications to your plan for the next day to incorporate time for your students to practice the skill.

Ultimately, your purpose for adding this part of the lesson plan is to measure how well your students have learned the lesson based on the activities you gave and the method you used to present the lesson. This assessment helps you wrap up your entire lesson plan and move on to the final part.

REFLECTION

This final part of your lesson plan is more for you than for your students. Typically, you won't be adding this part until you have carried out the lesson for the day. The reflection part of your lesson plan will give you a chance to think about (or reflect) the lessons you have planned, how you executed the lesson, how your students learned from your methods, and how you can improve lessons for the future.

This is the time when you strive to improve your methods to make you a better teacher and to provide your students with a better learning experience. While completing this part of your lesson plan, try to find the answers to these questions:

- Were your students able to achieve all of the learning objectives you have set for them?
- Were you able to accomplish all of the activities you planned within your estimated timeframe?
- Were there any activities that seemed too easy or too difficult for your students?
- Were your students interested and engaged in your lessons and activities?
- Was there any point during the lesson when you feel like you weren't prepared?
- Is there anything you would like to change in terms of how you delivered your lessons?

Basically, reflecting on these questions gives you an idea of how to handle your lessons and activities more efficiently in the future. When it's time for you to make the lesson plan for the next week, you can consider all of these improvements to make a more comprehensive lesson plan.

These are the fundamental components of a lesson plan. If your school provides you with a specific format to follow, you can still try to incorporate these components to ensure that the lesson plan you make is complete and provides high-impact learning. Keep practicing and soon, you will become a master at lesson planning.

6

DEALING WITH CHALLENGING STUDENTS

I n this final chapter, we will be focusing on one of the most difficult parts of being a teacher—dealing with challenging students. At some point in your career, you will face these kinds of students and if you don't know how to handle them, you might end up wanting to give up your teaching career altogether.

No matter how prepared you think you are, whether you're a new teacher filled with passion or you already have several years of experience to be proud of, you will come across difficult students who will make you feel totally unprepared. No matter what age group or level you are teaching, there will always be those difficult students who make school difficult for everyone, especially you. While the other students in your class might complain about these difficult students, you as the teacher must learn how to handle them effectively.

As the teacher, you shouldn't allow difficult students to have a negative impact on the rest of the class. Even worse, you shouldn't allow these students to influence others or you will end up with a whole class or misbehaving, disruptive, and disobedient students. Nobody wants that. To begin with, here are some basic tips to keep in mind:

Keep the lines of communication open

When it comes to difficult students, communication is key. You must communicate openly with the students and their parents. With this kind of problem, you and the student's parents will have to work together to make things better. Although you might be able to change the behaviors of the difficult student in school, your job becomes much easier if the strategies you use would also be applied (by the parents) at home.

Teach them about accountability

If you want a difficult student to understand that what they're doing is wrong, then you have to help them understand the concept of accountability. You can achieve this by establishing expectations and rules from the beginning. If the student blatantly disregards those rules, and they do it frequently, then it's time to introduce consequences. Once a student understands that they will have to deal with the consequences of their actions, you might start seeing a positive change in them.

Show genuine empathy

While it's much easier to lose your temper and make assumptions about why some students are being difficult, showing genuine empathy is much more effective. More often than not, students are difficult in school because they have underlying issues in their personal lives. If you can communicate openly with your students while showing them that you care, they might start opening up to you. When this happens, you might be able to help your students deal with their problems so that they won't act out in school.

Dealing with challenging students isn't an impossible task. For this issue, you must learn how to identify your problem students before you can find out how you can help them become better.

WHEN YOUR STUDENTS ARE YOUR BIGGEST CHALLENGE

When you have problematic students in your class, you will find yourself struggling or feeling frustrated because it's never easy to deal with such students. Of course, there are ways for you to influence their behavior. You can do this by establishing your authority without having to use heavy punishment and discipline.

Often, the most challenging students in your class are the ones who need the most love, empathy, and understanding. Most of these students are acting out because they are going through something either in their home or personal life—and they don't know how to deal with it. As a teacher, if you just scold these students or single them out in class all the time, they won't see your classroom as a safe space where they can learn new things and express themselves freely. Instead, they might just consider going to school as another problem that they have to deal with.

When you realize that your students are your problem, you have to dig down deep to find the strength to deal with them in the most patient, empathic, and loving ways. Although planning to deal with such students is a lot easier than actually applying the strategies you have planned, this isn't an impossible task. To become a great teacher, you should learn how to overcome the challenge of difficult students for your sake, their sake, and for the sake of all the other students in your class. Show your students that you genuinely care for them through the following ways:

- Do some digging so that you can understand the underlying cause of a student's bad or disruptive behavior. Once you discover this, it becomes easier to help your student cope with their problems.
- Set goals for how you will manage the difficult students in your class. Identify the difficult students then come up with a plan for how you will help them improve.
- As much as possible focus on using positive strategies instead of negative ones like punishments or criticism.

Staying positive will help your students realize that you want to help them improve. If you are starting to feel any negativity towards the challenging students in your class, try to manage those feelings by thinking about situations in your life when you might have acted the same way because you couldn't deal with your problems. This is an effective strategy that helps you put things into perspective.

- Never ignore or hide from such students. You should always let them know and feel that you are there. Your goal is to help them realize that even if you're the authority figure in the classroom, you are still there to help them out.

- Find ways to establish a connection with your students. After this, find ways to strengthen that connection until you have built a supportive student-teacher relationship. This will help your students feel more comfortable with you—and more willing to listen to what you have to say.

- Be your students' number one fan. No matter how small their achievements are in class, recognize them for it. Just make sure that the support and recognition you give are genuine as they can easily determine if you're just doing things for show.

- Instead of assuming the worst when you identify the challenging students in the class, try to assume the best. In doing this, you will change your own mindset to prepare you to handle difficult situations and difficult students better.

- Giving students the freedom to make choices in class is very effective in terms of encouraging them to learn. When dealing with challenging students, it's not enough to just give them choices—you should also learn how to respect the choices they have made.

- If a difficult student does something unacceptable in class, give a consequence for it. You won't necessarily be punishing them. You would just do something to make them realize that what they did wasn't right.

The most important thing to do when dealing with difficult students is to maintain consistency. Keep working hard to help your challenging students improve until you don't consider them as "challenging" anymore. Keep at it and you will soon see your whole class changing for the better.

TYPES OF CHALLENGING AND DISRUPTIVE STUDENTS

As a teacher, you will encounter different types of students who you might consider challenging or difficult. The problem with disruptive students is that they tend to affect those around them. Unless you can calm these students down and encourage them to follow the rules, the rest of the class won't be able to focus. Therefore, you should learn how to identify the most challenging students in your class before you do anything. The strategies you use to handle them would depend on what type of students they are and the level of disruptions they are causing in the class. The different types are:

Alpha Students

Alpha students are the ones who would provoke you just to see how far your limits are. With such students in the class, you would often experience power struggles, especially since alpha students tend to have other disruptive students behind them. Although it can be very tempting to engage in power play with these students, try to avoid it. Otherwise, you would just be giving these students exactly what they expect from you.

Argumentative Students

Argumentative students are a lot like alpha students, but they don't have a group of friends who support them. These students have a tendency to contradict you in class, which is a way for them to gain power over you. It's easy to get into arguments with such students, especially when they are also rude or disrespectful. Although you should find a way to nip this behavior in the bud as soon as possible, try to do it without showing blatant disrespect to the student too.

Brooding Students

Brooding students are also known as moody students, and they can be very disruptive, especially when they never want to participate in the class activities. If you notice this type of student in your class, then you should find ways to make them feel more interested. But if you have a student who suddenly becomes moody or brooding when they previously weren't, you might want to ask them what's wrong as they might be going through a difficult time in their life.

Clingy Students

Clingy students are very common when you are teaching young kids. They have a tendency to follow you around, or they would always ask you to help them with whatever activity they are doing. At the beginning of the class, you can expect a lot of clingy students. But after a few months, they should already feel confident enough to try doing things on their own. Otherwise, they would cause you and the rest of the class to feel distracted because they would keep calling out to you.

Inappropriate Students

Inappropriate students are more common with older students like those in high school or college. Typically, they would either act inappropriately towards you or towards the other students in the class. They might be overly flirtatious, they might make a lot of inappropriate jokes, or they might make a lot of lewd comments. While you and the rest of the class might ignore such students, in the beginning, you have to do something to change these behaviors if you see that they are already affecting those around them or if they are already disrupting the dynamics of your class.

Know-it-All Students

Know-it-all students are a lot like argumentative students but the difference is, they are simply overzealous or super excited about expressing themselves. They aren't interested in power play. Instead, they just want to show you that they know a lot of things. You may appreciate these types of students in the beginning but if you don't teach them to settle down and learn how to listen, they will start causing disruptions in your class. Still, you should show appreciation to the enthusiasm of these students—but also remind them that there is a time to talk and a time to listen.

Painfully Shy Students

Painfully shy students need a lot of encouragement and motivation to help bring them out of their shell. But if months have already passed, and they remain painfully shy and unwilling to participate, other students might start taking notice. To avoid bullying, you have to find ways to help these students get over their shyness. Of course, you shouldn't force them to do things that bring them out of their comfort zone. Instead, try to find out what they are interested in so that they will feel more willing to participate in the different activities you give in the class.

Resistant Students

Resistant students are the ones who just don't want to follow anything that you say. No matter what activity you give, they will refuse to participate. There are many reasons why students would end up becoming resistant. Some of them might feel bored with your activities, some might find the lessons too difficult, but they won't admit it while others just don't want to follow you because they don't like or trust you...yet. The best way to get through to these students is by getting to know them better. Establish a connection with your resistant students, and they might start responding positively to you.

Talkative Students

Talkative students are the ones who just can't seem to stop themselves from talking all throughout the class. Sometimes, solving this problem is as easy as moving the talkative student away from their friends. However, there are students who would keep on chatting with those around them no matter who they are sitting with. In such a case, you have to find a way to make these students understand that there is a time to talk and a time to listen. Also, you can put their love of talking to good use by allowing them to recite or report frequently. Hopefully, this will encourage the other students in your class to speak up more too.

Other Types of Students

Aside from the types of students mentioned above, there are other types of students who can cause disruptions even though they aren't as "challenging" as the rest. These include:

- **Disputers** who tend to cause trouble by disputing or debunking your authority, expertise or judgment just because they don't agree with you.
- **Late-comers** who always come in late and when they do, you and the rest of the class might lose your focus.
- **Gadget-users** who are glued to their smartphones and other devices. Because of this, they don't listen to you and other students might even start following their example.
- **Sleepers** who, although passively disruptive, send the wrong message to the other students. If you just allow your students to sleep in class, it shows that you don't mind this form of disrespect that they are showing you.
- **Threatening students** who try to intimidate you or other students through physical or verbal threats. When you have such students in the class, you have to put a stop to these behaviors immediately—and by any reasonable means necessary.

When it comes to challenging students, remember that not all disruptive behaviors stem from a lack of respect for you or from aggression towards you. There are many reasons why students act the way they do. This is why you should find out the reason behind your students' behavior first before you make a plan for how to deal with it.

COPING STRATEGIES TO HELP YOU OVERCOME THESE CHALLENGES

Having difficult, disruptive, and challenging students in your class can take up a lot of time and energy. Simply having a few of these students in a class can already make things extremely frustrating for you—and the other students will find it extremely difficult to focus. Therefore, you have to do something about it. Here are some tips for you:

Control your temper!

The first thing you have to do when dealing with difficult students is to remind yourself to keep your cool. Doing this might be very challenging, especially in the heat of the moment but learning how to control your temper will help you with all the other steps and strategies you have to do. Try to breathe deeply when you feel like you're about to explode at one of your students, who is trying to challenge you in front of everyone else.

If you feel like you can't control yourself any longer, step out of the class. Breathe deeply, count to ten, and go back inside to continue with the lesson. When you have given the rest of the class an activity to work on, approach the student, and ask them to step outside with you so that you can talk.

Create a plan of action

Once you have identified the challenging students in your class, the next thing to do is to discover why they are acting that way. This may take some time depending on how communicative the student is. After this, you can start creating a plan of action for how you will deal with your difficult students. Remember that each student is unique, even the challenging ones. Therefore, you may have to create several plans—one for each student you want to help improve.

Help your students feel safe in your class

If you want to get through to your students, you have to make them feel safe in your class first. Show your students that you genuinely care for them, you want to help them improve, and that you are willing to do what you can to help them solve their problems. This is an essential step, especially for students who are acting out because the other adults in their lives aren't showing them respect and authenticity. Once you have gained your student's trust, then you can start helping them out.

Just make sure that while you are establishing a connection with your student, you also draw the line. This ensures that your student won't take advantage of your kindness. When your student does something out of line, remind them that you are still the teacher and you expect them to follow the rules in class.

Praise your students when you see good changes

As you help your students improve, observe them carefully. If you see that they are trying to make an effort to change their behaviors, praise them for it! You don't have to wait for big gestures or huge improvements. Seeing simple acts that show that your students are going in the right direction are already enough to merit genuine praise from you. This will inspire and motivate them to keep going. Remember, notice progress, not perfection.

Never attack your students

As you learn how to control your temper, you should also learn how to respect your students no matter how difficult they are being. Never attack them for doing something in class. Even if a student doesn't show you respect, return their disrespect with firm but respectful disapproval. If you attack your students or meet their actions with the same negativity, this will only make things worse.

If a student has something to say, listen mindfully. You should learn the reason why they were behaving badly through your conversation. Never do things like sighing, crossing your arms or rolling your eyes. Instead, maintain eye contact while they listen so that you can determine the best course of action. Consider what your student has said, take a moment to think about their side, and try to come up with the best solution for the issue.

Give your students a chance to express themselves

At some point, you have to allow your disruptive students to express themselves and release their pent-up emotions. If you keep trying to prevent them from doing things or you keep saying, "no" to them, they might act out in different but equally negative ways. This is where your creativity comes in. Try to think of activities that your students will enjoy. Make sure these activities are related to your lessons, and they will help your students see that it's better to follow the rules instead of causing distractions in the class.

Don't give in to what your students want

Most disruptive students do things to get your attention. Then there are others who will try to push you to the limit just to get a reaction from you. Just as you would try to control your temper, try to control your actions so that you don't give in to what your students want. If you notice a student who just wants to get your attention, try to ignore them purposely. At least until they settle down. For those who are obviously trying to get a reaction out of you, try to do the opposite. Then go ahead and deal with their behaviors later on.

Deal with your challenging students as soon as possible

Finally, make sure to deal with the behavior as soon as possible. If you wait too long, your disruptive students will just continue their bad behaviors. What's worse, your other students might think that misbehaving and causing disruptions in class are okay.

Disruptive students are challenging, but you shouldn't ignore them. If you want to make things better for your students, then you have to deal with such behaviors right away. Throughout this chapter, you learned a lot of strategies to do just that. Think about these as you create your plan to make a positive change in your class.

CONCLUSION: BECOMING THE BEST TEACHER YOU CAN BE

When it comes to improving yourself to become the best teacher you can be, there is no time like the present. Now that you have reached the end of this book, it's time for you to start applying everything you have learned to your classroom. From start to finish, you have learned a wealth of information that you can use to teach yourself how to teach. In this valuable resource book, we started off with learning about the different types of learners. Since your students are your main priority as a teacher, getting to know them is key to becoming a great teacher. By discovering the learning styles of your students, you can come up with ways to give them the best learning experiences.

In the next chapter, you learned all about blended learning. This is a unique approach to teaching wherein you combine the best parts of traditional learning with the most innovative and relevant aspects of online learning. Online learning is a very important method, especially in this modern-day and age. You can further your learning by purchasing the second and third books that I have written which focus on learning all about online teaching, how to create online courses, and everything in between. These books are focused mainly on online learning and you will surely learn a lot more from them.

The next chapter was all about classroom management, a very important skill that you need to become an effective teacher. You learned all about disruptive behavior, the importance of classroom management, and several strategies to help you learn how to manage your classroom effectively while creating a fun learning environment for your students. Next up, you discovered the importance of inspiration, motivation, and how you can motivate your students to learn. This is another crucial aspect of the learning process because students need the motivation to help them learn effectively.

In the next chapter, we defined the art of lesson planning. After that, we went through the different parts of an effective lesson plan to help you understand what these parts involve and how you can create them. And in the last chapter, you learned how to deal with challenging students and how to cope with the frustrations they bring.

As you can plainly see, all of the concepts presented here will help improve all the aspects of your life as a teacher. As promised at the beginning of this book, you now have all the tools and practical knowledge you need to start becoming an inspiring and effective educator. Now, all that is left to do is to use the knowledge you have gained. It's time for you to start changing the lives of your students by teaching them in different ways.

If you enjoyed this book as much as I enjoyed writing it, please leave a review on Amazon. That way, other teachers who are yearning to make a positive change in their lives can also begin their journey to greatness.

Thank you so much for choosing this book to teach yourself valuable lessons. I hope you choose to continue your learning journey by purchasing the other books in the series. Good luck and may your passion bring inspiration to those around you.

Thank you for reading my book. If you have enjoyed reading it perhaps you would like to leave a star rating and a review for me on Amazon? It really helps support writers like myself create more books. You can leave a review for me by scanning the QR code below:

Thank you so much.

Selena Watts

REFERENCES

4 Blended Learning Models to Help Reach Students' Goals. (2018, August 17). *Classtime Blog.* https://www.classtime. com/blog/blended-learning-models/

4 Types of Learners in Education. (2017, October 12). Advancement Courses Blog. https://blog.advancementcourses. com/articles/4-types-of-learners-in-education/

Amada, G., & Smith, M. C. (1999). *Disruptive Classroom Behavior.* https://www.fullerton.edu/integrity/_resources/ pdfs/Disruptive%20Classroom%20Behavior.pdf

App, L. (2018, April 11). *The benefits of traditional education.* LearnX. https://learnxapp.com/blog/2018/04/11/the-benefits-of-traditional-education/

B, J. (2012, April 1). *4 Types of Problem Students and Strategies to Manage Them.* Busy Teacher. https://busyteacher.org/10587-4-types-of-problem-students-strategies-manage.html

Blake, C. (2015, April 28). *Cultivating Motivation: How to Help Students Love Learning.* Resilient Educator. https://resilienteducator.com/classroom-resources/cultivating-student-motivation/

Cabal, C. (2017). *How to Keep Your Students Motivated.* British Council. https://www.britishcouncil.org/voices-magazine/how-keep-your-students-motivated

CAE Team. (2018, June 4). *Why Do Students Prefer Blended Learning over Traditional Learning?* CAE. https://www.cae.net/why-students-prefer-blended-learning-over-traditional-learning/

cdadmin. (2020, January 11). *10 Different Types of Learners.* The Asian School. https://www.theasianschool.net/blog/types-of-learners/

Centre for Teaching Excellence, & Singapore Management University. (2019, June 27). *Lesson Planning In 6 Steps.* Bright Classroom Ideas. https://www.brightclassroomideas.com/lesson-planning-six-steps/

Cerdán, A. G. (2018, December 26). *Importance of Motivation: What Is It and Tips to Promote It.* CogniFit's Blog. https://blog.cognifit.com/importance-of-motivation-learning-tips/

Cox, J. (2019a, April 1). *Here's What You Need to Know About Lesson Plans.* ThoughtCo. https://www.thoughtco.com/what-is-a-lesson-plan-2081359

Cox, J. (2019b, October 22). *Tips for Handling Difficult Students.* ThoughtCo. https://www.thoughtco.com/tips-on-handling-difficult-students-2081545

Daniels, A. (2018, November 28). *What Is Considered Disruptive Behavior in a Classroom?* Hello Motherhood. https://www.hellomotherhood.com/what-is-considered-disruptive-behavior-in-a-classroom-4900126.html

De, B. (2018, February 4). *Traditional Learning Vs. Online Learning.* ELearning Industry. https://elearningindustry.com/traditional-learning-vs-online-learning

Dearborn, G. (2015). *Compassionate Discipline: Dealing with Difficult Students.* AMLE. https://www.amle.org/BrowsebyTopic/WhatsNew/WNDet/TabId/270/ArtMID/888/ArticleID/532/Compassionate-Discipline-Dealing-with-Difficult-Students.aspx

DeLong, M., & Winter, D. (2010, June 10). *Motivating Students.* Vanderbilt University. https://cft.vanderbilt.edu/guides-sub-pages/motivating-students/

Dominican University of California. (2017, November 23). *Be an Inspiring Teacher.* Dominican CA Online. https://

dominicancaonline.com/coaching-life-lessons/be-an-inspiring-teacher/

Einstein, A. (n.d.). *A Quote by Albert Einstein*. Goodreads. https://www.goodreads.com/quotes/253933-i-never-teach-my-pupils-i-only-attempt-to-provide

ELN.IO. (2018, March 3). *3 Reasons Why Lesson Planning is Important*. ELN Resources. https://www.eln.io/blog/3-reasons-lesson-planning

Elrick, L. (2018, August 9). *4 Types of Learning Styles: How to Accommodate a Diverse Group of Students*. Rasmussen College. https://www.rasmussen.edu/degrees/education/blog/types-of-learning-styles/

ERC Admin. (2017, January 23). *3 Reasons Why Traditional Classroom-Based Learning is Still King*. ERC. https://www.yourerc.com/blog/post/3-reasons-why-traditional-classroom-based-learning-is-still-king

Ferlazzo, L., & Sypnieski, K. H. (2019, December 9). *What Teachers Can Do to Boost Student Motivation*. Education Week. https://www.edweek.org/ew/collections/student-motivation-videos/what-teachers-can-do-to-boost-student.html

Fulton, J. (2018, September 20). *How to Get Your Class Under Control or Why Classroom Management is Important*. Classcraft Blog. https://www.classcraft.com/blog/features/why-classroom-management-is-important/

GoGuardian. (2019, August 21). *How to Write a Lesson Plan: Guide for Teachers.* GoGuardian. https://www.goguardian. com/resources/teachers/how-to-write-a-lesson-plan-a-teachers-guide/

Guido, M. (2018, September 20). *20 Classroom Management Strategies and Techniques [+ Downloadable List].* Prodigy. https://www.prodigygame.com/blog/classroom-management-strategies/

Guido, M. (2019, January 10). *How to Put the Six Blended Learning Models into Action [+ Examples & Download].* Prodigy. https://www.prodigygame.com/blog/six-blended-learning-models-examples-download/

Hurst, M. (2012). *The Importance of Motivation in an Educational Environment.* Study.Com. https://study.com/academy/lesson/the-importance-of-motivation-in-an-educational-environment.html

Johnston, T. (2018, September 6). *What is Classroom Management?* Palomar College. https://www2.palomar.edu/pages/tjohnston2/what-is-classroom-management/

Kardamis, L. (2014). *10 Ways to Motivate Your Students to Learn.* Teach 4 the Heart. https://teach4theheart.com/10-ways-to-motivate-your-students-to-learn/

Lathan, J. (2018, January 5). *An Educator's Guide to Teaching Styles & Learning Styles.* University of San Diego. https://onlinedegrees.sandiego.edu/teaching-to-every-students-unique-learning-style/

Lawless, C. (2019, January 17). *What is Blended Learning?* LearnUpon. https://www.learnupon.com/blog/what-is-blended-learning/

Linsin, M. (2011, April 23). *The 7 Rules Of Handling Difficult Students.* Smart Classroom Management. https://www.smartclassroommanagement.com/2011/04/23/7-rules-of-handling-difficult-students/

Literacy Planet. (2017, October 9). *How to Engage the 7 Types of Learners in your Classroom.* Literacy Planet. https://www.literacyplanet.com/au/news/engage-7-types-learners-classroom/

McClymont, G. (2016, August 8). *7 Components of an Effective Classroom Lesson Plan.* Owlcation. https://owlcation.com/academia/Components-of-an-Effective-Classroom-Lesson-Plan

Mccutchen, M. (2019, October 30). *How to build a great lesson plan (with a template!).* Classcraft Blog. https://www.classcraft.com/blog/features/how-to-build-a-great-lesson-plan-with-a-template/

Mendler, A. (2017, November 9). *6 Great Strategies For Dealing With 'Difficult' Students.* TeachThought. https://www.teachthought.com/pedagogy/growing-closer-to-your-most-challenging-students/

Ministry of Education, Guyana. (2015). *Why Classroom Management Is Important.* Ministry of Education, Guyana. https://www.education.gov.gy/web/index.php/teachers/tips-for-teaching/item/1651-why-classroom-management-is-important

Motivating Students. (2019). Teach.Com. https://teach.com/what/teachers-change-lives/motivating-students/

Movchan, S. (2018). *What Makes a Good Learning Environment.* Raccoon Gang. https://raccoongang.com/blog/what-makes-good-learning-environment/

Mulvahill, E. (2018a, February 27). *What is Classroom Management?* WeAreTeachers. https://www.weareteachers.com/what-is-classroom-management/

Mulvahill, E. (2018b, July 3). *Understanding Intrinsic vs. Extrinsic Motivation in the Classroom.* WeAreTeachers. https://www.weareteachers.com/understanding-intrinsic-vs-extrinsic-motivation-in-the-classroom/

Murray, B. P. (2019). *The New Teacher's Guide to Creating Lesson Plans.* Scholastic. https://www.scholastic.com/

teachers/articles/teaching-content/new-teachers-guide-creating-lesson-plans/

Owen, J. (2019, July 25). *Ultimate Guide To Blended Learning.* Education Technology. https://edtechnology.co.uk/latest-news/ultimate-guide-to-blended-learning/

Phibzia. (2016, March 23). *Classroom Connections - Creating a Fun Learning Environment for Students.* Beneylu Pssst. https://beneylu.com/pssst/en/classroom-connections-creating-a-fun-learning-environment/

Pivotal Education. (n.d.). *Why is Motivation So Important for Learning Success?* Pivotal Education Behavior Specialists. https://pivotaleducation.com/hidden-trainer-area/training-online-resources/why-is-motivation-so-important-for-learning-success/

Post, G. (2017, March 9). *How to Spark Intrinsic Motivation in Your Students.* Teach.Com. https://teach.com/blog/how-to-spark-intrinsic-motivation-in-your-students/

Powell, W., & Kusuma-Powell, O. (2011). *How to Teach Now.* ASCD. http://www.ascd.org/publications/books/111011/chapters/Knowing-Our-Students-as-Learners.aspx

Read + Write Learner. (2017, February 8). Learning Styles 101; Learning Styles 101. https://learningstyles101com.wordpress.com/blog/read-write-learner/

Reis, R. (n.d.). *How to Deal with Difficult Students.* Stanford University. https://tomprof.stanford.edu/posting/1542

Riskey, E. (2016, September). *Dealing with Difficult Students - Classroom Management Tips.* Study.Com. https://study.com/blog/dealing-with-difficult-students-classroom-management-tips.html

Rosell, C. D. (2020a, June 11). *Introducing Blended Learning into a Traditional Classroom.* CAE. https://www.cae.net/how-to-introduce-blended-learning-to-a-traditional-classroom/

Rosell, C. D. (2020b, June 25). *Blended Learning in the Classroom: Five Creative Ways to Use It.* CAE. https://www.cae.net/five-ways-to-incorporate-blended-learning-methods/

SchoolDays. (n.d.). *Five Types of Challenging Behaviour Every Teacher Finds in the Classroom.* SchoolDays. https://www.schooldays.ie/articles/five-types-of-challenging-behaviour-every-teacher-finds-in-the-classroom

Shafer, M. (2017, November 30). *What to Do for the Most Challenging Students in Your Class.* Teaching Channel. https://www.teachingchannel.com/blog/challenging-students

Shalaway, L. (2019). *25 Sure-Fire Strategies for Handling Difficult Students.* Scholastic. https://www.scholastic.com/teachers/articles/teaching-content/25-sure-fire-strategies-handling-difficult-students/

Smith, M. (2019, January 16). *Understanding The 7 Types Of Learning Styles.* Mindvalley Blog. https://blog.mindvalley.com/types-of-learning-styles/

Somji, R. (2018, April 17). *Teaching Strategies for the 8 Different Learning Styles.* VirtualSpeech; VirtualSpeech. https://virtualspeech.com/blog/teaching-strategies-different-learning-styles

Stauffer, B. (2019, September 1). *What Is a Lesson Plan and How Do You Make One?* Applied Education Systems. https://www.aeseducation.com/blog/what-is-a-lesson-plan

Teach.com. (2019). *Learning Styles.* Teach.Com. https://teach.com/what/teachers-know/learning-styles/

TeachThought Staff. (2012, December 11). *21 Simple Ideas To Improve Student Motivation.* TeachThought. https://www.teachthought.com/pedagogy/21-simple-ideas-to-improve-student-motivatio/

Team, U. (2015, September 9). *14 Best Techniques to Increase Students' Motivation.* Unicheck Blog. https://unicheck.com/blog/motivating-students

Terada, Y. (2019, August 7). *8 Proactive Classroom Management Tips.* Edutopia. https://www.edutopia.org/article/8-proactive-classroom-management-tips

The Chalk Team. (2019, February 26). *10 Tips for Keeping Your Teachers Motivated | Chalk.* Chalk. https://www.chalk.

com/resources/tips-keep-teachers-motivated/

The Share Team. (n.d.). *3 Examples of Effective Classroom Management.* Resilient Educator. https://resilienteducator. com/classroom-resources/3-examples-of-effective-classroom-management/

Time4Learning. (2019, October 22). *Different Learning Styles.* Time4Learning. https://www.time4learning.com/learning-styles/

University of Hawaii. (n.d.). *Disruptive Student Behavior in the Classroom.* HILO. Retrieved July 20, 2020, from https:// hilo.hawaii.edu/studentaffairs/conduct/disruption.php

University of Massachusetts Dartmouth. (2019). *How to Accommodate Different Learning Styles.* Umass Dartmouth. https://www.umassd.edu/dss/resources/faculty--staff/how-to-teach-and-accommodate/how-to-accommodate-different-learning-styles/

University of Nebraska. (2019). *Twenty Tips on Motivating Students | Graduate Studies | Nebraska.* University of Nebraska–Lincoln. https://www.unl.edu/gradstudies/current/teaching/motivating

University of Texas. (2015, December 15). *Transforming School into a Fun Learning Environment.* UTA Online. https://academicpartnerships.uta.edu/articles/education/transforming-school-into-a-fun-learning-environment.aspx

Unlu, V. (2017, December 11). *Managing Disruptive Behaviour in the Classroom*. World of Better Learning. https://www.cambridge.org/elt/blog/2017/12/11/managing-disruptive-behaviour-in-the-classroom/

VARK Learn. (2020). *Read/Write Strategies*. VARK - A Guide to Learning Preferences. https://vark-learn.com/strategies/readwrite-strategies/

West, C. (2017). *The 8 Learning Styles: Which One Works for You?* Visme. https://visme.co/blog/8-learning-styles/

West, D. (2018, June 18). *How to Pare Your Lesson Plans Down to the Essentials*. The Art of Education University. https://theartofeducation.edu/2018/06/18/how-to-pare-your-lesson-plans-down-to-the-essentials/

What are the Benefits of Blended Learning? (n.d.). Digital Marketing Institute. Retrieved July 20, 2020, from https://digitalmarketinginstitute.com/blog/what-are-the-benefits-of-blended-learning

Whittenberger, R. (2014, October 22). *5 Easy Ways To Use Blended Learning In Your Classroom*. Ving. https://blog.vingapp.com/5-easy-ways-use-blended-learning-classroom/

wikiHow. (2006, July 11). *Make a Lesson Plan*. WikiHow. https://www.wikihow.com/Make-a-Lesson-Plan

Wikipedia Contributors. (2019, March 4). *Blended learning*. Wikipedia; Wikimedia Foundation. https://en.wikipedia.org/wiki/Blended_learning

Wilcox, L. (2018, June 4). *Top 5 Strategies for Motivating Students*. NBPTS. https://www.nbpts.org/top-5-strategies-for-motivating-students/

Wilson, C. (2016, February 6). *6 Ways Teachers Are Using Blended Learning*. TeachThought. https://www.teachthought.com/learning/6-blended-learning-models-platforms/

Winjigo. (n.d.). *How to Apply Blended Learning in the Classroom?* Winjigo. Retrieved July 20, 2020, from https://www.winjigo.com/how-to-apply-blended-learning-in-the-classroom/

Yussif. (2019, May 9). *Why is Classroom Management Important?* Classroom Management Expert. https://classroommanagementexpert.com/blog/what-is-the-importance-of-classroom-management/

Zook, C. (2018, November 15). *What Is Blended Learning?* Applied Education Systems. https://www.aeseducation.com/blog/what-is-blended-learning

Made in the USA
Monee, IL
14 February 2021

60493864R00100